MAGNIFICENT MINDS

MAGNIFICENT MINDS

2ND EDITION

*Seventeen Pioneering Women
in Science and Medicine*

Pendred Noyce

TUMBLEHOME, INC.
BOSTON, MASSACHUSETTS

Dedication

To Sabrina, who surprised us with her love of research,
and to all young discoverers like her.

BOOK DESIGN BY JEANNE ABBOUD

Library of Congress Control Number: 2020951730
ISBN: 9781943431649

CONTENTS

FOREWORD

Women have participated in the development of the sciences since the late sixteenth century, although their contributions have long gone unacknowledged. Written in an engaging style, this timely text by Pendred Noyce creates a portrait gallery of women who were pioneers in science, engineering, mathematics, and medicine. This volume and the one to follow, *Remarkable Minds,* deserve the close attention of the education community. Moreover, for anyone seeking insights into a life in science, the recurring patterns that appear throughout these narratives are essential.

The essays in the author's book do not simply recount interesting stories nor do they offer routine biographies describing women's accomplishments. Instead, women's lives are clearly situated in the context of their time and the society in which they lived. For example, Italy in the eighteenth century did not impose the constraints on women that were commonplace in most other European countries. The lack of opportunities in education for women—in some cases active parental and institutional discouragement—which continued to some extent into the twentieth century, is a theme that appears repeatedly throughout these accounts. In the case of published works, many pre-nineteenth-century French women, preferring to remain anonymous or pseudonymous, did not place their names on the title pages of their works. It is also worth noting that when writing about the private lives of these women, the author focuses on marriage and family, matters that continue to present concerns for young people who may be considering a career in science.

The women's interactions with the scientific establishments of their times varied from being confined to the role of an independent scholar, working as an unpaid assistant, and in some fortunate cases being mentored in their chosen field. In the end, despite gender bias and other obstacles, these extraordinary women, who are the subjects of this book and the one that follows, persevered and created their own individual paths to success.

As the curators who organized the 2013 exhibition "Extraordinary Women in Science & Medicine: Four Centuries of Achievement" at the Grolier Club and authored the book of the same name, we hope these volumes by Pendred Noyce will be noticed and read by young people, teachers, and important members of the education community. We are delighted to see our work in its second life and in the service of encouraging education and learning.

Ronald K. Smeltzer
Paulette Rose
Robert J. Ruben

ACKNOWLEDGMENTS

This book exists because of six people. The first three are Ronald Smeltzer, Robert Ruben, and Paulette Rose, who created an exhibition on scientific women at the Grolier Club in New York. Over two years they researched thirty-two women and gathered written artifacts to display. Once the exhibition opened, they led tours for school groups and casual visitors, acting as raconteurs and guides. They also put together an exhibition catalogue entitled *Extraordinary Women in Science and Medicine: Four Centuries of Achievement*. The catalogue has been the starting point for all the chapters in this book. Moreover, the curators have repeatedly reviewed these chapters to help me avoid errors; any that remain are my own.

The fourth person is Steve Rasmussen, former publisher of Key Curriculum Press. Steve and his wife Felicia happened upon the Grolier exhibition on a visit to New York. Thinking that the subject matter of the exhibition would make a good book for young people, Steve connected Ronald Smeltzer with me at Tumblehome Learning. Thus this book was born.

The final two people are Eugene and Irena Bonte. Through their foundation, they provided support for the writing, illustration, and printing of this book.

I would be remiss not to mention another important source. Sharon McGrayne's book, *Nobel Prize Women in Science*, provided inspiration, guidance, and depth as I learned about seven of the women in this book. For those who want to learn more, McGrayne's book would be an excellent place to start.

Finally, I am grateful to the women portrayed in this book for their leadership in science. I loved learning about them, and I look forward to writing about their sister scientists in a companion volume, *Remarkable Minds*.

INTRODUCTION

What does a French midwife share with an Austrian physicist, or a flighty English noblewoman with an American admiral? The seventeen women profiled in this book span four centuries of history in eight countries across three continents. They found their way into this volume because of their variety, because they have interesting stories to tell, and because they made fundamental contributions to the world's knowledge of science. Some of them saw themselves as pioneers opening the way for other women to follow; others did not. Yet overall, their stories reveal themes that are still relevant for young women, and even young men, entering the sciences today.

The seventeen women are a diverse group who challenge still-existing stereotypes about women in science and engineering. For example, the women had interesting love lives. Six of the women never married—one, Gertrude Elion, tragically lost her fiancé to heart disease—but eleven did. Six of the women married fellow scientists or medical practitioners, and four of the marriages involved close scientific partnerships. Romantic scandal swirled around at least three of the women, Ada Byron, Sofia Kovalevskaya, and Marie Curie.

More than half of the women found themselves displaced, exiled, or shaken by war. Louise Bourgeois Boursier started her profession as midwife to support her family after losing all her possessions to an invader. Maria Cunitz and her husband spent their lives moving from place to place to avoid anti-Protestant attacks. Florence Nightingale launched her famous career in the theater of the Crimean War. The Japanese invasion of her homeland and subsequent civil war kept Chien-Shiung Wu from returning to the China of her birth. For all of these women, their devotion to science provided an anchor in uncertain times.

Most of the women in this volume came from families who valued education. For six of them, their fathers were their first teachers and advocates. Laura Bassi's father proudly raised her as an "exceptional woman" who could debate with men as an equal; Emmy Noether's father was a professor of mathematics who helped her audit his colleagues' classes in a university not yet open to women. In one case, that of Ada Byron, a mother insisted on her daughter learning mathematics as a way to protect her against the possibility of inheriting madness from her father.

After their good start at home, these women often found academic high schools and universities closed to them. Six of the women, from Mary Putnam Jacobi to Chien-Shiung Wu, left their home countries to pursue their education abroad in France, Germany, or the United

States. Even the generation who had no trouble entering universities learned to their dismay that graduate programs or research positions discriminated against women. Chien-Shiung Wu decided not to attend graduate school at the University of Michigan when she learned that women were not allowed in the student union. Gertrude Elion worked as a secretary and a substitute teacher until the departure of men for World War II opened research positions in industry to women. Barbara McClintock left university life for good when she was told she would never be promoted. If anything, women were expected to use their education to teach in a girls' school, as Marie Curie did, or perhaps a women's university, as Dorothy Hodgkin did at Somerville College, or as Grace Hopper did before she joined the Navy.

Many of the women worked as unpaid volunteers or saw themselves paid much less than their male colleagues. The exceptions include Louise Bourgeois Boursier, who made a very good living as a midwife until male physicians forced her out of the profession, and Laura Bassi, who in the 1770s became the highest paid professor at the University of Bologna. But Marie Curie, Lise Meitner, and Emmy Noether all worked at first as unpaid assistants to family members or colleagues. For others, including Maria Cunitz, Marie Meurdrac, and Ada Byron, the question of earning money from their work never arose: they pursued their science because they loved it and felt they had something to offer.

Some of the women, even those whose fathers initially delighted in educating them, faced strong family opposition when they wanted to pursue a career. So opposed was Sofia Kovalevskaya's father to the idea of higher education for women that Sophie had to elope to escape his strictures. Florence Nightingale reached her thirties before she finally broke free of her disapproving Victorian family to obtain training as a nurse. Mary Putnam Jacobi's father offered her $250 to give up her idea of pursuing medicine. Barbara McClintock's mother initially forbade her to attend college, fearing that too much education would prevent her from finding a husband.

Many of the women found themselves passed over for advancement and recognition because the world at large assumed that the men they worked with were the true researchers. Maria Cunitz's physician husband had to write a preface to her astronomy text assuring readers that the work was hers alone. Ada Byron labored to bring Charles Babbage's innovations to the public eye; which of them should be credited with writing the first computer program is still a matter of debate. Lise Meitner and Chien-Shiung Wu were passed over by the Nobel Prize committee because their work was considered less important than their collaborators'.

Despite the barriers they faced, all seventeen of these women achieved astonishing insights and made significant contributions to the progress of science. The independence and originality of their work increased across the centuries. Louise Boursier and Marie Meurdrac contributed to science primarily by gathering their hard-earned expertise into books for other women. Maria Cunitz translated Kepler's *Rudolphine Tables* into a form much easier for other astronomers to use. Laura Bassi organized an experimental physics course and performed original experiments of her own. The next twelve women profiled in the book all performed significant original research, making fundamental contributions to mathematics, nuclear physics, genetics, computer science, structural chemistry, and drug discovery. Patricia Bath, the last woman profiled, used her expertise to confound her colleagues with a new and important invention. How did they manage to do so?

The structural barriers the women faced were often offset by help from individual men who served as mentors, friends, and colleagues. Institutions barred or belittled them, but professors took them on as pupils; fellow students befriended them; and colleagues sought them out. Lise Meitner and Emmy Noether would not have made it out of Hitler's Germany alive without the support of foreign, mostly male, colleagues.

Family members also provided financial support. The fathers of Florence Nightingale and Lise Meitner subsidized them with living allowances. Dorothy Hodgkin's aunt paid for her education. Marie Curie and her sister took turns contributing to each other's university expenses.

The most profound reason for these women's successes, however, was their own curiosity and their inner drive to understand. Many of them shared a sense of service, and many more were motivated by a desire to make their lives worthwhile. They knew that a lifetime confined to the traditional roles of mother, wife, or society woman could never be enough for them. Their minds were alive and begged to be challenged. Science, with its never-ending questions and its sudden moments of clarity, delighted them. They loved to immerse themselves in the work of discovery. Though sometimes shy, timid, or uncertain, the seventeen women in this book persisted until they found or created arenas where their magnificent minds could freely play.

Timeline | 1563-1636

Birth of Louise Bourgeois Boursier | 1563

1572 | St. Bartholomew's Day Massacre
begins French Wars of Religion

ST. BARTHOLOMEW'S
DAY MASSACRE

Louise Boursier flees to Paris | 1589

1598 | Boursier passes midwife examination

1598 | Edict of Nantes protects Protestants

Boursier delivers | 1601
the Queen's first son

LOUIS XIII

1609 | Boursier publishes her
book on obstetrics

Henry IV | 1610
assassinated

1620 | Pilgrims land at Plymouth

First marriage of Maria Cunitz | 1623

William Harvey describes | 1628
circulation of the blood

EMBARKATION OF
THE PILGRIMS

Death of Boursier | 1636
at age 73

WILLIAM HARVEY

1 | *Midwife to the Queen*

Louise Bourgeois Boursier

1563-1636 | *France*

On October 31, 1589, finding herself in the pathway of an invading army, Louise Bourgeois Boursier packed up what valuables she could carry and fled with her mother and three small children to safety within the walls of Paris. That night, soldiers of Henry of Navarre, Protestant claimant to the throne of France, attacked her hometown of St. Germain. In the riot of victory, Henry's soldiers destroyed or stole everything they could lay hands on.

Louise's husband, the barber-surgeon Martin Boursier, was away on military duty, so Louise had to find a way to earn money in Paris. Like any daughter of a well-to-do family, she had learned reading, writing, and needlework at home. Now Louise turned to her needlework, selling her sewing pieces to neighbors. But she couldn't make enough to support the family. Bit by bit, Louise Bourgeois and her mother sold off the few pieces of furniture they had saved from the invaders.

LOUISE BOURGEOIS BOURSIER

HENRY OF NAVARRE AT WAR

Louise Bourgeois Boursier lived during the **Wars of Religion**, *which pitted Catholics against Protestants all over Europe.* **Henry of Navarre**, *who later became King Henry IV, was baptized a Catholic but raised a Protestant by his mother. This meant that when he became heir to the throne, the Catholic League sent Catholic armies against him. By 1593, despite winning many battles, Henry of Navarre had still not conquered Paris. Finally he took the pragmatic step of converting to Catholicism. Tradition attributes to him the famous phrase, "Paris is well worth a Mass." As a Catholic, Henry was accepted as king.*

By most accounts, Henry IV was a good king who cared about his subjects. In 1598 he issued the Edict of Nantes, which for the first time prevented persecution of the Protestant Huguenots. Perhaps in retribution for this act of tolerance, in May 1610 Henry was stabbed to death by a Catholic fanatic.

At some point Louise Bourgeois began to consider another profession. Hadn't her husband lived as an apprentice for many years in the house of the king's surgeon, Ambroise Paré? Bourgeois began to study Paré's works for tidbits on pregnancy and childbirth. Before long she offered to help deliver the baby of her porter's wife. Soon she was acting as midwife to women, rich or poor, all over the Latin Quarter of Paris.

> *One in ten French women died in childbirth.*

Midwifery in France in the sixteenth century was a demanding profession. One in ten French women died in childbirth, most often from bleeding or infection. (By contrast, in the United States today, only twenty-one women die for every 100,000 live births.) France responded in part by setting up a licensing system for midwives. In 1598, Bourgeois presented herself for examination. By this time Henry of Navarre had become King Henry IV of France, and Bourgeois' surgeon husband had been home from the wars for several years. The board that examined Louise Bourgeois Boursier included one physician, two surgeons, and two midwives. One of the midwives questioned Bourgeois closely about her husband's profession. Then she turned to the other and said, "By God, my friend, my heart tells me nothing good for us, since she is the wife of a surgeon. She gets on with the physicians like thieves at a fair." Despite this woman's fears that Louise Bourgeois would take the side of physicians against midwives, Bourgeois passed her exam and gained an official license to practice as a "sworn midwife."

Partly through her good relations with physicians, all of whom were male, Louise Bourgeois rose to become midwife first to noblewomen and finally to Henry IV's new queen, Marie de Medici. In 1601 she delivered the royal couple's first son, the future king Louis XIII. After the birth, two hundred people swarmed into the room. When Bourgeois protested that the queen needed quiet, the king admonished her, "Hush, hush, midwife, do not be angry at all, this child is everyone's, everyone must rejoice."

In all, Louise Bourgeois Boursier delivered five royal children. During the last two months of each of the queen's confinements, Bourgeois lived like a maidservant, eating meals with the other servants and riding in the back of the queen's coach. But unlike a servant, she was paid royally for her service. For each prince she delivered, she received ten times a midwife's usual annual earnings, and for each princess, six times. And when not attending the queen, Bourgeois continued to practice among other women of the court as well as the middle and working class women of the Latin Quarter.

HENRY IV

FRONTISPIECE OF BOURSIER'S BOOK ON CHILDBIRTH

"... the first woman practicing my art to pick up the pen."

By 1609, Louise Bourgeois had delivered two thousand babies, and she decided it was time to write a book. Proudly, she claimed that she was "the first woman practicing my art to pick up the pen." Published in 1609, *Diverse Observations on Sterility, Loss of the Ovum, Fertility, Childbirth, Women's Ailments, and Newborns* was promptly translated into other European languages. Bourgeois added to it throughout her life, and the book became the essential reference book for midwives for the next fifty years.

In her book, Bourgeois drew on two sources: her understanding of the humoral basis of medicine as practiced by the leading physicians of the day and her own practical experience. She described how to handle both normal and risky deliveries, what to do when the mother starts to bleed heavily, how to deliver twins, how to turn a baby in the uterus, and how to deliver a baby from a dying mother. She wrote about how to handle a retained placenta. She discussed how to keep

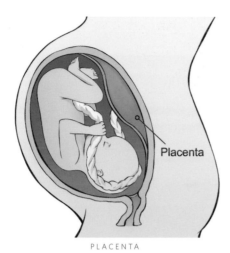

PLACENTA

The **placenta** is an organ found only in mammals. It connects the umbilical cord of the developing fetus to the wall of the mother's uterus. Filled with blood vessels, the placenta allows the exchange of nutrients, gases, and waste between mother and child. Usually, the placenta is delivered at the end of labor, several minutes after the baby is born. If in childbirth the placenta breaks, or if part of it is left behind, it can cause heavy bleeding or later infection.

a calm and safe environment during and after labor and how to care for both mother and baby immediately after the birth.

In 1610, a Catholic fanatic assassinated Henry IV. His death meant that Bourgeois delivered no more royal princes, but she continued to attend noble ladies. Then disaster struck. One of her patients, sister-in-law of the young King Louis XIII, died of fever a week after delivering a child. Though the young woman had been sick during much of her pregnancy, the physicians attending her deflected blame from themselves by blaming the midwife for her death. They performed an autopsy that showed peritonitis or widespread infection in the abdomen. The cause, they implied, was a bit of retained placenta in the uterus.

Louise Bourgeois did not submit quietly to the physicians' judgment. In a written response, she pointed out that several physicians present after the birth had examined the placenta and proclaimed it whole. Moreover, the autopsy showed the infection and dead loops of bowel on the side *opposite* the supposed retained bit of placenta. She scolded the physicians who had performed the autopsy, writing,

> Based on your report you have no knowledge of the placenta and the womb of the woman, either before or after delivery . . . In order to know the secrets of women's maladies, it is necessary to have worked with midwives, and to have assisted at several deliveries, as your great Master and legislator Hippocrates did, who in treating women's maladies, consulted midwives, deferring to their judgment.

Needless to say, the royal physicians did not appreciate having an uppity woman cast back on them the blame for a death in the royal family. Before her response, Bourgeois might have been allowed to retire quietly. Now one physician, writing anonymously, set out to crush her:

No longer involve yourself in responding to Doctors. . . . Do not glorify yourself with the name of Midwife. Foresee what can be drawn from your presumption and your writings, and no longer talk with such haughtiness against the men who are more practiced and more happy than you in the profession that you do.

The author's actual arguments against Bourgeois' points about the autopsy were weak, and a modern examination of the evidence absolves her of responsibility for the princess's death. Still, in publishing her angry rebuttal, Bourgeois had gone too far. None of her doctor friends came publicly to her defense. Her days delivering babies at court were over.

> *"There has never been complete mastery in medicine . . ."*

Bourgeois spent the rest of her days writing about the midwife's art and delivering babies in more modest households. She died in 1636 at the age of 73. Throughout her life, she had continued to learn, writing, "There has never been complete mastery in medicine, nor in all that depends on it; one must learn until the last day of one's life."

A brave and independent woman, Louise Bourgeois Boursier did not hesitate to discuss and collaborate as a near equal with the leading physicians of her day. She learned from books, but she learned even more from her careful observation of thousands of births. Moreover, she shared what she learned in books written in the vernacular, not in the Latin of physicians, to benefit other midwives and anyone working with pregnancy and childbirth. Unlike some of the devout men of her time, she did not believe that the pain of labor served to help women atone for the sins of the first woman, Eve. Instead, she sought to decrease women's pain and increase the safety of childbirth. Besides helping to launch the field of scientific medicine, her works undoubtedly saved the lives of thousands of women and infants.

Timeline | 1601-1668

LOUISE BOURSIER

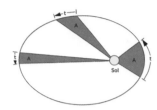

KEPLER'S LAWS

Tycho Brahe dies | 1601

1604 | *Birth of Maria Cunitz?*

Louise Boursier's book on obstetrics | 1609

1609 | *Kepler's Laws of Planetary Motion*

Birth of Maria Cunitz? | 1610

1610 | *Galileo discovers four moons of Jupiter*

John Napier invents logarithms | 1614

GALILEO

Kepler's Rudolphine Tables | 1620

1623 | *Marries a lawyer*

First husband dies | 1626

1629 | *Flees to Leignitz*

Marries Elias von Löwen | 1630

1618 – 1648 *Thirty Years' War in Europe*

ISAAC NEWTON'S
TELESCOPE

Publishes Beneficent Urania | 1650

Fire destroys Cunitz's papers | 1655

Death of Maria Cunitz | 1664

1668 | *Isaac Newton builds first reflecting telescope*

2 | *Figuring the Stars*

Maria Cunitz

1610?-1664 | *Poland and Germany*

She watched the stars all night and slept all day, neglecting her household duties. So reported Maria Cunitz's first biographer. Luckily, Cunitz had a physician husband who shared her interest in the stars. Her contemporaries called her the greatest female astronomer since Hypatia. A current essayist has named her "the greatest astronomer between Kepler and Huygens."

> *"The daylight hours she spent, for the most part, asleep."*

Maria Cunitz is one of the women in this book about whom least is known, in part because of a fire that destroyed her papers and letters later in her life. But like many of the other women scientists, she benefited from a supportive husband and suffered uprooting because of war.

Born in Wohlau, in the western part of what later became Poland, Maria Cunitz considered herself German. Her home was in Silesia, part of the Holy Roman Empire. Her birthdate fell approximately fifty years after Louise Bourgeois Boursier's, between 1604 and 1610, with the strongest evidence pointing toward the later date. Her Protestant family was "illustrious and learned;" her father was a physician and her mother the daughter of a scientist. As a teenager, Maria knew seven languages: German, Latin, Greek, Hebrew, Italian, French, and Polish. She played music, painted, and did needlework, but she also learned history and mathematics.

DEFENESTRATION OF PRAGUE

*The **Thirty Years' War** (1618-1648) was a struggle over religion and power. Tension between Protestants and Catholics in Central Europe broke into open conflict after Protestants in Prague threw Catholic king-to-be Ferdinand II's councilors out of a council house window in Prague. This famous "defenestration of Prague" led to a revolt that spread through the multiple German states and on to the whole continent of Europe, including Spain, Sweden, and France. Prolonged and destructive, the war with its accompanying disease and starvation led to a significant population decline in the German states.*

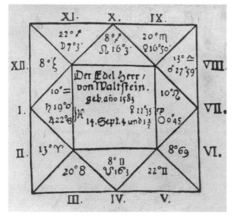

HOROSCOPE BY KEPLER

MARIA CUNITZ STATUE

In 1623—evidence suggests that she was only thirteen and a half—Maria married a lawyer, David von Gerstmann. Following his death three years later, she lived at home and carried on her studies. One of her interests was astrology, which required precise predictions of the position of celestial objects at any given time. Astrology was a great interest of physicians at the time, because the position of the stars at the moment of birth was felt to influence human health and disease. The only other practical purpose of astronomy at the time was calculating precise dates for religious celebrations.

Maria's efforts in astrology came to the attention of Dr. Elias von Löwen, who began to advise her by letter, even teaching her trigonometry to assist with her lengthy calculations. The correspondents became friends, and von Löwen showed his affection for the family in 1629, when the Holy Roman Emperor Ferdinand's Thirty Years' War against Protestantism arrived at the Cunitzes' doorstep. Maria's three sisters converted to Catholicism and remained in place, but Maria and her parents fled to the city of Leignitz. It appears that von Löwen accompanied them on their flight. The next year, after the death of Maria's father, Maria and Elias married. The couple had three sons.

PTOLEMAIC SYSTEM, BY CELLARI.
THIS IS HOW ASTRONOMERS UNDERSTOOD THE PLANETARY SYSTEM BEFORE COPERNICUS AND KEPLER

Not long after the marriage, the von Löwen family was forced to flee again, east to Pitschen, near the Polish border. A few years later, the couple escaped across the river into Poland, where, although they never abandoned their Protestant faith, they came under the protection of a Cistercian convent. Later, in his introduction to Maria's book, Elias expressed his gratitude to the nuns, who "showed [us] every kindness, benevolence, and favor, and a peaceful and safe stay."

Sometime after their marriage, Elias introduced Maria to Kepler's *Rudolphine Tables*. The history of these tables dated back more than fifty years to observations made by Tycho Brahe and his assistants on the island of Hven in the Danish Sound. For twenty-four years, Tycho's group used the finest instruments of the time to make thousands of detailed observations as part of a grand plan to reform astronomy. Then, after a falling-out with King Christian IV of Denmark, Tycho moved his books and instruments to Prague, where he became Imperial Mathematician. Emperor Rudolph II gave Tycho permission to name his observations the *Rudolphine Tables*, but Tycho died before the tables could be completed.

TYCHO BRAHE

After Tycho's death in 1601, Johannes Kepler inherited responsibility for publishing the *Rudolphine Tables*. Consumed by creating his new theories for planetary motion, Kepler delayed publication. Only after finally completing the formulation of his theories in 1605 did Kepler

KEPLER

In 1609, based on the astronomical observations of Tycho Brahe, **Johannes Kepler** *published his first two* **Laws of Planetary Motion***:*

1. *The orbit of every planet is an ellipse with the Sun at one of the two foci.*
2. *A line segment connecting the planet to the Sun sweeps out equal areas in equal intervals of time. This second or Area Law means that during its orbit, a planet moves faster when it is closer to the Sun.*

turn to deriving the orbits of the planets by applying his theories to Tycho's observations. The calculations involved were lengthy and tedious. In 1618, after years of frustrating labor, Kepler was delighted to hear about logarithms, invented by John Napier in 1614. Using logarithms, Kepler was able to convert complex multiplication problems into simpler problems of addition. Six years of calculation later, Kepler finished his reworking of the *Rudolphine Tables*. From the tables, in theory, one could calculate *ephemerides (eh-feh-MARE-id-deeze)*, tables giving the future positions of planets or comets. Kepler and his son-in-law computed such tables for 1621-1636, but few other astronomers were willing to take on the burdensome calculations required.

Maria Cunitz was an exception. Like others before her, she found the use of logarithms and the repetitive calculations required for predicting astronomical movements almost unbearably time-consuming. But rather than abandon her work, she decided to convert Kepler's tables into something simpler and more usable, "though" as her husband wrote, "the labor to do so was immense." The historian of science Noel Swerdlow notes that calculating a planetary position using Kepler's tables takes at least an hour. Cunitz devised a simpler method and painstakingly converted the tables, correcting Kepler's errors—and introducing a few others—along the way.

In 1648, the political situation had settled enough that Cunitz and von Löwen were able to move back to Pitschen, where she redoubled her studies. Finally, in 1650, after almost twenty years of labor, Maria and Elias published her work. Cunitz named her book *Beneficent Urania (Urania Propitia)* after Urania, Muse of Astronomy. Five hundred pages long, the book includes 300 pages of number tables. In his preface entitled "Husband to the Reader," von Löwen assured readers that, unlikely as it might seem, the work was indeed written by a woman working alone.

Cunitz wrote two hundred pages in both Latin and German explaining how to use the tables. In her remarkable introduction, she defended this decision, saying that although writing in Latin, the language of scholars, was a necessity, "the German Nation abounds in those of abilities suited to astronomical practice although often lacking knowledge of Latin." Moreover, she wrote, "It is agreed by the opinion of foreigners also that the Nation claims a great part of our labors as its own." To her mind, the German nation, which had driven her into exile, deserved her service. Finally, she argued, by writing in two languages she could undercut scoundrels who "translate works of some note into another language, with the authors not knowing, not consulted, not willing, rather with their names entirely suppressed." She made her own translation to avoid plagiarism.

Part I of *Beneficent Urania* includes tables of trigonometry and a multitude of astronomical measurements. Part II consists of tables of mean motions and corrections for the sun, planets, and moon. Part III provides tables for calculating eclipses, along with others predicting the motions and illumination of the moon. In the book Cunitz clearly described planets orbiting the sun according to the Copernican theory and demonstrating the elliptical orbits Kepler had described.

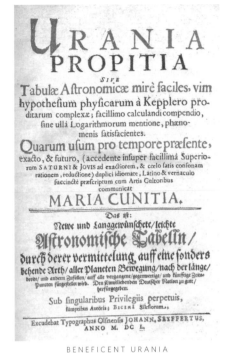

BENEFICENT URANIA

Publication of *Beneficent Urania* brought Cunitz fame among scholars of northern Europe. She began corresponding with numerous astronomers, including Hevelius, considered among the most distinguished theoretical and observational astronomers of the day. Unfortunately, in 1655 a fire in Pitschen destroyed the family house and library, including papers, instruments, and von Löwen's supplies for concocting medicines. Little is known of the remainder of Cunitz's life until her death at the age of fifty-four.

> *"The Nation claims a great part of our labor as its own."*

Ronald Smeltzer calls Maria Cunitz "probably the most advanced scholar of mathematical astronomy in her time." Noel Swerdlow writes that *Beneficent Urania* "has the distinction of being the earliest surviving scientific work on the highest technical level of its age." By mastering the mathematics of her time and applying it to scientific questions of the day, Cunitz prefigured the accomplishments of many of the women in this volume.

Timeline | 1603-1687

Queen Elizabeth I of England dies | 1603

1607 | Jamestown founded in Virginia

Birth of Marie | 1610? Meurdrac

QUEEN ELIZABETH

Meurdrac marries | 1625 Henri de Vibrac

1626 | Dutch traders purchase Manhattan

William Harvey | 1628 describes circulation of the blood

DUTCH TRADERS PURCHASE MANHATTAN

1637 | Descartes publishes Discours de la Méthode

English Civil War begins | 1642
Louis XIV | 1643 ascends throne of France

LOUIS XIV

1662 | Boyle proposes Ideal Gas Law

Death of | 1664 Maria Cunitz

1666 | Meurdrac publishes Easy and Useful Chemistry

Death of Marie Meurdrac | 1680

1685 | Louis XIV revokes the Edict of Nantes

Newton's Laws of Motion | 1687

EASY AND USEFUL CHEMISTRY

3 | *Chemistry for Women*

Marie Meurdrac

1610?-1680 | *France*

Seventeenth century science grew from two medieval roots, the mystical and the practical. Chemistry sprang from alchemy, a human attempt to understand, explore, and control the elements of nature. Alchemists developed complex theories to try to explain the hidden qualities and unexpected transformations of matter, and they often wrote in an esoteric or mystical language intelligible only to other initiates. But chemistry also has a humbler origin. Probably since before the beginning of civilization, people, most often mothers, have tried to find cures for family ailments. Marie Meurdrac, sometimes considered the first woman chemist, straddled both traditions, but what she cared most about was being of service to poor women.

Marie was one of two girls born into a French landholding family living in a suburb of Paris. Her father was a notary who added to his properties during Marie's childhood. While Marie's older sister Catherine loved to ride, hunt, and fence, the limited records we have suggest that even

ALCHEMIST'S WORKSHOP

GROSBOIS

as a girl, Marie was more serious. She served as godmother to several village children. In 1625, at around fifteen years of age, she married Henri de Vibrac, captain of the guard for Charles de Valois, the Duke of Angoulême. After her marriage, Marie Meurdrac lived in the duke's chateau of Grosbois, where she was befriended by the Countess de Guiche.

Apparently the widowed countess shared Meurdrac's interest in both chemistry and service to the community. With the countess as her benefactress and patron, Meurdrac taught herself practical chemistry. She read the works of alchemists and contemporary chemists. Not contented with her theoretical reading alone, Meurdrac also performed experiments, mixing and extracting substances and testing their effects. Her aim was to improve the lives of women, so she focused on home remedies and beauty products, carefully recording recipes for her concoctions.

"not to lose memory of the knowledge that I had acquired"

After many years of serving her own neighborhood, Marie had the daring idea of writing a book. Her introduction describes how she debated the question of whether doing so was proper for a woman. She wrote:

> When I began this small treatise, it was for my sole satisfaction, so as not to lose memory of the knowledge that I had acquired by means of long toil, and by divers experiments repeated several times.

For two years, Meurdrac, lacking the brash confidence of Louise Bourgeois Boursier half a century earlier, wrestled with whether to publish. The common scholarly belief at the time was that too much learning would make women pedantic, irritating, and ridiculous. Presenting a work to the public, Meurdrac feared, would expose her to censure. She knew of no other woman who had written about the emerging science of chemistry. Finally, though, she concluded:

> [that] I am not the first woman to have placed something under the press, that mind has no sex, and if the minds of women were cultivated like those of men, and if we employed as much time and money in their instruction, [we] could become their equal.

Meurdrac wrote *La Chymie Charitable et Facile, en Faveur des Dames* (*Benevolent and Easy Chemistry for the Benefit of Ladies*, 1666) in French for the common reader. She urged the reader to do as she did, and provide the remedies she described without charge to the poor.

In seventeenth century France, the medical hierarchy started at the top with physicians, who studied theory and taught anatomy but did not touch actual patients. Surgeons, on the next rung down, dirtied their hands with surgery. Barbers, lower yet, could assist surgeons when they were not shaving beards or cutting hair. Apothecaries were allowed to mix and dispense medicines. Women, however, were forbidden entry to any of these professions. It was understood that wives and mothers might gather herbs and follow "recipe books" handed down in their families to dose their own children; but women, being considered uneducated and ignorant, were forbidden from selling their remedies. While Marie Meurdrac's work had its roots in these humble recipe books, she asserted a firm

ALCHEMICAL SYMBOLS

WOMAN IN 18TH CENTURY CHEMISTRY LAB,
COURTESY OF RONALD SMELTZER

Here are two of Marie Meurdrac's recipes, for helping to make hair grow and to prevent smallpox scars:

Take two handfuls of clematis roots, two handfuls of hemp roots, and two handfuls of tender cabbage stalks. Let them dry, burn them and make a solution from the ashes. Before washing your hair with this solution you must rub your head with honey and repeat the process for three days.

Pigeon blood, drained from under the wing, prevents scarring from smallpox if applied to the emerging sores with a feather three or four times a day.

grounding in knowledge based on her study of medical and chemical theories. Whether these theories had any scientific validity is beside the point. Meurdrac's recipes carried greater authority because of them.

Meurdrac's book contained no pictures or index, but it did include a chart of 106 alchemical symbols, which she sought to demystify, and a detailed table of contents. Her book had six parts. First Meurdrac discussed chemical operations and apparatus, such as vessels, crucibles, measuring weights, retorts, and a furnace. Furnaces, she pointed out, are not allowed to everyone, but the reader should not despair, because a tripod surrounded by bricks or a corner of the hearth would serve as well.

Next Meurdrac described substances extracted from plants, followed by those derived from animals. She went on to discuss inorganic chemistry, including the study of metals. In the fifth section, Meurdrac wrote about how to make substances useful in medicine, "with several tested remedies" including treatments for headache, earache, and toothache. Her final section, comprising a quarter of the book, specifically addressed products for women's beauty and health. Her cosmetic concoctions included perfumes, tooth whiteners, face and hand creams, cleansers, sunscreens, hair dyes, and preparations for itching skin.

Many of Meurdrac's recipes for home use were remarkably simple, allowing them to be concocted easily in the kitchen. For example, she recommended using an alcoholic extract of rosemary for cleansing the skin. Doing so, she suggested, might prolong life or even cure blindness. Meurdrac claimed to have copied the recipe from one used by the emperor Charles V's daughter, who had used it to cure her gout.

Meurdrac's conception of chemical theory was firmly rooted in the knowledge current in her time. She followed the Renaissance physician and alchemist Paracelsus (1493-1541) in stating that the three basic elements were mercury, representing the spirit; sulfur, representing the soul; and salt, representing the body.

At the same time, she expressed doubt that other chemists had created soluble compounds of gold and silver as they claimed. She argued that

those who have written about these matters are less attached to demonstration than to speculation, in which one is often deceived, for theory and practice are ordinarily different, and action instructs us far better than contemplation.

With these words, Meurdrac aligned herself more closely with the practical wisdom of hands-on experimentation than with the lofty theorizing of scholars. Of primary importance, she asserted, was the practical ability to separate and isolate substances from mixtures—still one of the major tasks of chemistry.

Although Meurdrac made no notable independent discoveries, her book does demonstrate that she was a competent apothecary and practical chemist. Moreover, her intuition that the book would fill a real need proved correct. *La Chymie des Dames* by "Damoiselle M.M." experienced immediate success, with five French editions, several German editions, and at least one Italian edition. Even the faculty of medicine in Paris endorsed the book, finding in it "nothing but what will be useful to the public."

USEFUL AND EASY CHEMISTRY FOR LADIES

> *"Action instructs us far better than contemplation."*

Like Louise Bourgeois, Marie Meurdrac believed that women, properly educated, could make a contribution to medical knowledge. Again like Bourgeois, she carved out a role for herself serving the needs of women in particular. Unlike Bourgeois, she was not driven by financial necessity and did not challenge the male medical hierarchy. But by hesitantly asserting her right to teach what she had learned, Marie Meurdrac struck an early blow for women's rights to learn and practice science.

Timeline | 1706-1789

Birth of Ben Franklin | 1706

Birth of Laura Bassi | 1711

1712 | First commercial use of a steam engine

Death of Louis XIV, France's Sun King | 1714

1724 | Russian science academy created at St. Petersburg

Receives doctorate in Bologna | 1732

1738 | Marries Giuseppe Veratti

Begins offering physics lectures at home | 1744

1745 | Invention of Leyden jar, the first capacitor

Ben Franklin shows that lightning is electrical | 1751

1749 | Death of Émilie du Châtelet, French physicist

1755 | Lisbon earthquake kills 100,000

BEN FRANKLIN

French Encyclopedia is completed | 1765

1773 | Boston Tea Party

BOSTON TEA PARTY

Priestley discovers oxygen | 1774

Becomes chair of experimental physics | 1776

1776 | American Declaration of Independence

1778 | Death of Laura Bassi

French Revolution | 1789

FRENCH REVOLUTION

4 | *A Physicist of Bologna*

Laura Bassi

1711-1778 | *Italy*

In April 1732, a young woman named Laura Bassi rode in a carriage to Bologna's Palazzo Pubblico. Two noblewomen attended her, although she was only a lawyer's daughter. As she entered the palace's grand salon, nobles, scholars, cardinals, bishops, doctors, and lawyers rose from their seats. Then the lovely and modest twenty-year old Bassi took her place to defend the theses that would win her one of the first doctoral degrees ever awarded to a woman in Europe.

Bologna, a proud city-state directly ruled by the Pope, had founded Europe's first university in 1088. But by the 1700s, the university's fame was fading. Publicly awarding a degree to a woman was bound to attract attention. Officials made the most of Laura Bassi's carefully staged public performance.

Not all scholars believed that women could think and contribute at a level comparable to men. "La Querelle des Femmes," a public debate about women's nature and capability, had been raging at least since the scholar Christiane de Pisan began writing essays on the topic in 1405. Women, some men argued, were naturally corrupt, and their only hope of salvation was to stay at home, where they should concentrate on being meek and loving. Meanwhile, a handful of scholarly women argued that if women received a proper education, they could enter the public sphere and demon-

SEAL OF UNIVERSITY OF BOLOGNA

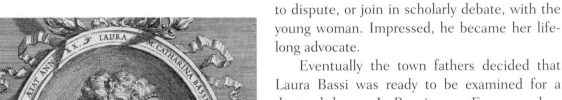

> *"Fluids women require to perform their primary reproductive function leave their physical fibers too weak and flaccid to sustain concentrated activity in the brain, thereby precluding women from serious thought and analysis."*
>
> – Giovanni Volpi (1686-1766), professor of philosophy, University of Padua.

strate an intellect equal to any man's. Against the background of this debate, the university fathers expected Laura Bassi's thesis defense to attract international notice.

Bassi was already known as a prodigy to many of the people in the room. Her father, a lawyer, had sought out the best teachers for her. At the age of five she began to study Latin, French, and arithmetic. When she was thirteen, her father engaged the family doctor to tutor her in logic, metaphysics, and optics. Soon Laura's father began inviting scholars to evenings at his home so Laura could engage them in debate.

Members of Bologna's Academy of Sciences attended these evenings, and in March 1732 they invited Bassi to join the Academy. Archbishop Lambertini, the future Pope Benedict XIV, also came to dispute, or join in scholarly debate, with the young woman. Impressed, he became her life-long advocate.

LAURA BASSI

Eventually the town fathers decided that Laura Bassi was ready to be examined for a doctoral degree. In Renaissance Europe, a doctoral thesis did not present original research. Rather, the candidate prepared to discuss questions about accepted knowledge and thought. Laura Bassi prepared forty-nine theses. Six covered logic, sixteen metaphysics, and nine the "Nature of Being, Reason, God and the Angels." Her tutor wanted her to discuss ethics for the remaining eighteen theses, but Laura gently insisted on preparing in physics instead. In front of her seven examiners, she held forth on matter, motion, and meteors.

The performance was a triumph. Laura Bassi received a silver crown, a book, a ring, an ermine mantle, and the degree of doctor of philosophy. Citizens wrote poems in her honor. A jeweler prepared her a silver and pewter medal. She was fêted at special dinners, and in October she gave her first university lecture, in which she argued that the philosopher's duty was to deduce laws of nature from phenomena that could be observed experimentally.

After the first flurry of activity, most citizens of Bologna expected Bassi to settle into the accepted role of an "exceptional woman": she should follow quiet literary pursuits. Noble families called on her to write Latin sonnets for births and weddings. On her own, Bassi studied calculus and physics, but she was not invited to Academy meetings, and after her first honorary lecture at the university, no one expected her to lecture again. Instead, in return for the honors bestowed on her, she was expected to remain virtuous, single, and feminine.

> *"I have chosen a person . . . I was certain would not deviate me."*

Laura Bassi had other ideas. For one thing, in 1738 she decided to marry. As husband she chose a fellow member of the Academy of Sciences, the physician Giuseppe Veratti. To many of her scholarly admirers, the choice seemed ill fated. Now she would have to turn from pursuits of the mind to the womanly drudgery of the body. After all, it was well known that reproductive fluids in women weakened the brain. Laura Bassi was throwing away everything about her that was special. One colleague wrote, "You have stained your glory." But Bassi was having none of it. With a husband, she reasoned, she would be able to attend Academy meetings and keep up with new scientific knowledge. She wrote of her husband, "I have chosen a person . . . I was certain would not deviate me."

In the years that followed, Laura Bassi bore nine—or maybe twelve—children. Four boys and one girl survived infancy. Despite her family duties, Bassi refused to retire into home life. She continued to lecture, giving at first only one lesson per semester, then, later, regular classes and lectures on anatomy. She received a raise. Around

FRONTISPIECE OF THE FRENCH ENCYCLOPEDIA

The **Enlightenment** or **Age of Reason** in Europe began in the late seventeenth and early eighteenth centuries. It was an intellectual movement that valued individual reason over traditional knowledge. Whereas Renaissance scholars had looked to classical writers like Aristotle or Galen for wisdom, Enlightenment scholars looked to logic, observable evidence, and the scientific method. Laura Bassi's focus on experimental rather than theoretical physics exemplified this new way of thinking.

18TH CENTURY EXPERIMENT
IN ELECTRICITY,
COURTESY OF RONALD SMELTZER

*The **Leyden jar**, invented in 1745-46, made studying electricity much easier than before. The Leyden jar is a simple capacitor that stores static electricity by piling up opposing charges on either side of an insulator like glass. To charge the capacitor, the experimenter turns a "friction machine," a ball of glass or sulfur that rubs against a cloth or the experimenter's hands. The friction of this rubbing action pulls off some electrons, which then travel through a metal chain or bar to the foil lining the inside of the jar.*

When the gap between the jar's inside and outside lining is bridged, the sudden discharge of electricity leads to a visible spark and a shock.

this time, perhaps with the help of Lambertini, now a cardinal, Bassi gained permission to read works forbidden by the church, such as the writings of Copernicus, Kepler, and Galileo. Increasingly, she grew dissatisfied with the theoretical approach to science favored by the university. Besides Aristotle, Galen, and Descartes, she wanted to learn and talk about new experiments done by Galileo, Boyle, and Newton.

In 1744, when she was thirty-two, Laura Bassi and her husband Giuseppe Veratti began offering regular physics lessons in their home. Veratti did physics demonstrations while Bassi provided the mathematics and directed the overall course. Over time, the couple built a state-of-the art physics laboratory, complete with books, articles, lenses, prisms, and electrical equipment that they bought, received as gifts, or built. They taught about forces and motion, electricity, gases, air purity, oxygen, and how the body works. Soon their audience included not just young male students, but visiting scholars.

In 1745, Pope Benedict XIV decided to stir up scholarship in Bologna's sleepy Academy of Science. To do so, he created a special subgroup called the Benedettini. This chosen group of twenty-four scientists would each be required to prepare and present one original paper each year. All twenty-four scientists were men. One of them was Giuseppe Veratti, Bassi's husband. Joining this group would mean an opportunity to interact with men

EXPERIMENTING WITH A LEYDEN JAR

working on real experimental science, and Bassi was not going to pass it up. Through an intermediary, she wrote to ask for help from her old champion, the Pope. Let him add a twenty-fifth scholar to the group, she pleaded. He did.

Over the next thirty-one years, Laura Bassi presented thirty-one dissertations to the Benedettini. She presented even in years when she was having babies and in years when she was ill. Most of her manuscripts have been lost, but we know their topics. She wrote about water, its pressure and flow; the behavior of gases in high humidity; bubbles; fire. Starting in 1761, she wrote about electricity. Her writings were based on experiments she carried out, sometimes with Veratti's help, sometimes on her own. And while her husband's papers were purely descriptive, Bassi's included carefully worked out mathematics.

POPE BENEDICT XIV

Her work with the Benedettini only increased Laura Bassi's renown. She corresponded with scientists all over Italy and Europe. She became involved in disputes over how electricity worked. Her home laboratory became a test bed for electrical experiments and debate. Intrigued by the work of Benjamin Franklin, Bassi was disappointed when the city of Bologna rejected the use of lightning rods. She also helped young scholars design and run their own experiments. She proposed using ash rich in iron as a new dye. She helped calculate the force released by gunpowder and described the shattering of glass.

Over time, Laura Bassi became the most highly paid faculty member at the University of Bologna. In 1776, when she was sixty-four years old, the post of chair of the physics department fell open. As she had for several years, Bassi argued for splitting the department into a theoretical and an experimental department. One administrator wrote that this was the chance "finally to satisfy, if one ever can, the demands of Signora Laura Bassi, who . . . has asked for this for well over three Years . . ." The university appointed Laura Bassi chair of experimental physics, and they made her husband her assistant. Bassi served in this position until her death in 1778 at the age of 66. Her husband Giuseppe Verlatti succeeded her as chair of experimental physics at the University of Bologna.

Bassi was one of the first women ever to make a living as a professional scientist. She interacted with male scientists as an equal in the institutions that supported science, including the University of Bologna and the Academy of Sciences. Although she advised other women and advocated for educational opportunities, she remained an "exceptional woman" rather than a role model that other women could easily follow. She played an important role in helping to spread the ideas and methods of experimental physics through Europe, and some of her students went on to make important scientific contributions of their own.

Timeline | 1791-1871

Birth of Charles Babbage | 1791

JANE AUSTEN

NAPOLEON

1812 | Napoleon invades Russia

Jane Austen publishes Pride and Prejudice | 1813

Napoleon defeated at Waterloo | 1815

1815 | Birth of Augusta Ada Byron

1818 | Mary Shelley publishes Frankenstein

Lord Byron dies in Greece | 1824

1829 | First electric motor

Ada meets | 1832
Charles Babbage

1835 | Marries William King

1843 | Publishes her Notes on
Babbage's Analytical Engine

MOBY DICK

Herman Melville publishes Moby-Dick | 1851

1852 | Death of Ada Lovelace

Charge of the Light Brigade in | 1854
the Crimean War

1861-65 | American Civil War

CIVIL WAR

Death of Charles Babbage | 1871

5 | *A Loom that Weaves Numbers*

Augusta Ada Byron, Countess of Lovelace

1815-1852 | *England*

Augusta Ada Byron, later the Countess Lovelace, lived a life both colorful and controversial. Daughter of a Romantic poet and a strait-laced, mathematically-minded high society woman, Ada Lovelace sought to create a kind of "poetical science." She was flirtatious, flighty, and brilliant, and like Emilie Du Châtelet, who translated Isaac Newton's *Principia Mathematica* into French, she devoted herself to translating the ideas of a visionary male to the public. Some consider her to have been the first computer programmer.

ADA BYRON, COUNTESS LOVELACE

Ada was born in London on December 10, 1815. She was the only legitimate child of the poet Lord Byron, who had married Ada's mother in January of that year. Byron referred to Ada's mother, a young woman of good family named Annabella Milbanke, as "The Princess of Parallelograms." His baby girl, he said, was "the child of love—though born in bitterness, and nurtured in convulsion." The bitterness began during Annabella's pregnancy, when Byron's drunken rages made his young wife believe he was going mad. Before long, Lady Byron also became convinced of an incestuous affair between the poet and his half-sister Augusta Leigh. A few weeks after Ada's birth, Lady Byron demanded a separation from her husband and full custody of the baby, threatening Byron with exposure if he refused. Byron left England in April 1816, never to see his daughter again. As for Lady Byron, she dedicated herself to wiping out any trace of Byron's "mad, bad" influence on her daughter's outlook or character. Ada was not allowed even to see a portrait of her father until she reached the age of twenty.

Lord Byron wrote home that he would like his daughter to learn music and Italian, but Lady Byron's program for Ada's education focused on mathematics, which she hoped would give her daughter the mental discipline to overcome any strain of madness inherited from her moody, tempestuous father. Lady Byron hired and dismissed a series of governesses, personally taking over her daughter's education during any gaps. A harsh teacher, she required Ada to lie perfectly still for long periods as a way of overcoming restlessness. From the age of four, if Ada did not perform well, she was placed in a closet until she reformed. After one such punishment, the child dutifully wrote in her journal, "I was rather foolish in saying that I did not like arithmetic. . . . The sums can be done better, if I tried, than they are." On Sundays, lessons were more fun: Ada was allowed to build objects of her own design with blocks.

The absent Lord Byron died of the flu in Greece at the age of thirty-six. He had always kept a picture of Ada on his desk, and according to his valet, his last words were, "Oh, my poor dear child! My dear Ada! My God, could I have seen her! Give her my blessing." Ada, eight years old at the time, wept at the news, but she had no real conception of who her father was.

The following year, Lady Byron took Ada for a grand, fifteen-month tour of Europe. Organ music and the Alps made a great impression on the young girl. Before long, however, she found herself installed once more in the English countryside, while her mother traveled for health cures and philanthropic missions. Left alone, Ada played with her cat Puff and began, at the age of twelve, to dream of building a flying machine. She designed a "thing in the form of a horse with a steam engine in the inside so . . . as to move an immense pair of wings," and mapped out a book called *Flyology* to share her findings on the wing anatomy of birds. But when Lady Byron reprimanded her by letter for neglecting her studies, Ada obediently took down the ropes and pulleys she had installed in her flying room and returned to work.

At age thirteen, Ada fell ill with measles, which led to temporary paralysis and then to three years as a bedridden invalid. Lady Byron urged her daughter to use the opportunity to concentrate on her studies, which expanded from mathematics to include chemistry, Latin, shorthand, and music. Not only her mother, but three of her mother's friends, whom Ada dubbed "the three Furies," watched over her. When she finally arose from her bed three years later, overweight and hobbling on crutches, Ada eluded the three Furies' oversight long enough to carry on a love affair with one of her tutors. Mr. Turner was abruptly dismissed and Ada was subjected to scathing sermons from her mother's friends.

Whatever her disappointment at the departure of Mr. Turner, Ada quickly found a new passion: learning to play the guitar from a Spanish count. Her mother, meanwhile, presented her daughter at court and continued to battle her romantic strain by encouraging her mathematical studies. She connected Ada first with Mary Somerville, an expert and author of a book on mathematical astronomy, and then with Augustus De Morgan, a prominent mathematician and logician. Lady

Byron also set up meetings for her daughter with various London scientists, preferably gentlemen of leisure and independent means. When Ada was seventeen, one of the gentlemen whom mother and daughter visited was the mathematician, inventor, and mechanical engineer, Charles Babbage.

CHARLES BABBAGE

At forty-two, Babbage was a professor of mathematics at Cambridge who devoted less attention to his teaching than to his interests in mechanical dolls, games of chance, economic arguments, printing, and machines. Twenty years earlier, Babbage had fretted that a table of logarithms calculated by hand was full of errors; he set himself the challenge of figuring out mechanical ways to improve such calculations. In 1823 Babbage received a government grant to build a machine, the Difference Engine, to more efficiently calculate polynomials and other algebraic expressions. By 1833, when Ada Byron met him, the Difference Engine was twenty-nine inches tall, and built of rotating gears and wheels marked with numbers. The machine was still unfinished, because the project had lost its government funding and Babbage had fallen out with the machinist responsible for building it. Nevertheless, he demonstrated the Engine to visitors, and Ada Byron was one of the few to understand both its working and its potential. Although her mother considered the Engine "the whim of the moment," Ada's interest struck deep enough that she began a regular correspondence with Babbage. Several years later, the correspondence ripened into collaboration.

BABBAGE'S DIFFERENCE ENGINE, LONDON MUSEUM OF SCIENCE

COMPUTER SCIENCE

Calculating Differences

Babbage's Difference Engine exploited the fact that the problem of finding subsequent terms in any polynomial can be converted to an addition problem. A polynomial is an expression of the form

$$ax^n + bx^{n-1} + cx^{n-2} + ... + hx + g$$

*The degree of the polynomial is the value of its highest exponent, in this case **n**. To calculate the differences, construct a table with n + 2 columns. For example, to calculate terms in the expression $3x^2 + 2x + 6$, construct a table with 4 columns.*

x=	$3x^2+2x+6$	first difference	second difference
0	6		
1	11	5	
2	22	11	6
3	39	17	6
4			6

*Calculate the value of the expression for the first few values of x. In the next column calculate the **differences** between those values, and in the next column, calculate the **second differences** or difference between those differences. For a polynomial of degree two, you will find that the second difference is always the same; for a polynomial of degree five, it will be the fifth difference that is always the same.*

Wherever you find it, that constant difference allows you to work backward. In our example, for x = 4, we find the first difference by adding 6 to 17, getting 23. To find the value of the expression when x = 4, we then add 23 to 39, getting 62. Checking, we find that $3(4^2) + 2(4) + 6$ is equal to 48 + 8 + 6, which is equal to 62. The method of differences has allowed us to convert a multiplication problem into an addition problem.

At eighteen, Ada visited the north of England, where she and her mother toured ribbon factories, printers, and rug factories. Ada took note of the punched cards used to control patterns created by the Jacquard looms.

Ada also tutored two daughters of one of her mother's friends, teaching them the use of a compass and protractor and the beauties of a direct mathematical proof. She urged them to visualize their problems, saying that she did not count herself as truly knowing a mathematical concept "until I can imagine to myself a figure in the air, and go through the construction & demonstration without any book or assistance whatever."

In 1835, when she was almost twenty, Ada married William King, a quiet and intelligent young man who three years later inherited the title Earl of Lovelace, making his wife the Countess Lovelace. Together the couple had three children, Byron, Annabella, and Ralph Gordon. The young countess continued her musical and mathematical studies, focusing on the harp, trigonometry, and calculus. When in the country, she rode horseback for her still-fragile health; when in the city, she attended balls and opera.

Meanwhile, Babbage was devising the idea for a new and more versatile machine, one which could not just do calculations but remember them and compare different quantities. This new machine he dubbed the Analytical Engine. Ada Lovelace yearned to help him. In 1841, now twenty-five, she wrote to him, "If ever I could be worthy or capable of being *used* by you, my head will be yours . . . You have always been a kind and real & most invaluable friend to *me*; and I would that I could in any way repay it, though I scarcely dare so exalt myself as to hope however humbly, that I can ever be intellectually worthy to attempt serving *you*." A few days later, she wrote less modestly to another family friend, "I have on my mind most strongly the

A TAPESTRY PORTRAIT OF JACQUARD,
WOVEN ON ONE OF HIS LOOMS

Jacquard Looms

Joseph Marie Charles, nicknamed Jacquard, was a French weaver and inventor whose mechanical loom was first displayed in 1801 at an industrial exhibition in Paris. A string of punched cards linked together with threads regulated the loom's operation. Each card gave instructions for one row of weaving. The position of the holes determined which vertical or warp threads were raised to allow the horizontal, or weft, thread to pass through the loom. The long string of cards looped, making a continuously repeating pattern. Jacquard looms inspired the punch cards in Babbage's engines as well as later computers.

JACQUARD LOOM

impression that Heaven has allotted me some peculiar intellectual-moral mission to perform."

The following year, Charles Babbage provided her with that mission. After eight years of work on his Analytical Engine, Babbage had described it in a seminar in Turin before a gathering of Italian engineers and philosophers. One member of the audience, L.F. Menebrea, reported the presentation in an obscure Swiss journal, and Babbage was interested in having the article translated from French into English. He turned to Ada, who seized on the project with enthusiasm. Soon, though, Babbage suggested more. Ada had seen how her friends and acquaintances struggled to understand Babbage's earlier work. Could she find a way, by adding explanatory notes of her own, to make his vision clearer?

In 1843, Ada Lovelace's translation appeared. Her notes, published only under the initials A.A.L., were three times the length of the original paper. Ada not only

> *"The Analytical Engine has no pretentions whatever to originate anything. It can do whatever we know how to order it to perform."*

explained the Engine's mechanism, she gave examples of what it could and could not do. As when teaching her neighbor's daughters, she used metaphor to help her reader envision what she wished to convey. "The Analytical Engine weaves algebraic patterns," she wrote, "just as the Jacquard loom weaves flowers and leaves." She stressed that the Engine could not initiate anything for itself, but could only do "whatever we know how to order it to perform." Then she went on to describe several fundamental concepts of computer programming. She described conditional branching—asking the Engine to make decisions by comparing numbers. She offered a scheme and a code for letting the machine operate with symbols as well as numbers, and she suggested that by using symbols, "the engine might compose . . . music of any degree of complexity." She also discussed the importance of using code recursively in what are now known as loops.

Babbage was so impressed by an early draft of Lovelace's Notes that he wrote to her, "All this was impossible for you to know by intuition and the more I read your notes the more surprised I am at them and regret not having earlier explored so rich a vein of the noblest metal." He referred to her as his "Enchantress of Numbers." Babbage was satisfied, but Lovelace wanted to take her Notes one step further.

In order to demonstrate the Engine's power, Lovelace conceived the idea of showing how it could solve problems not previously solved by hand. She pestered Babbage to explain how to perform a set of complicated algebraic operations to find what are known as Bernoulli numbers. In his letters, Babbage showed her the algebraic manipulations required. Lovelace identified an important error in his formulas and then set about translating them into specific step-by-step instructions for the Engine to carry out. This set of instructions has been regarded as the first computer program. Unfortunately, the program remained theoretical, because Babbage never succeeded in building his Analytical Engine.

Ada Lovelace's publication of her Notes in 1843 was the peak of her mathematical and scientific career. However, the notes were not widely read, and soon a return of various physical ailments put Lovelace under doctor's orders. Her mother, Lady Byron, still dominated her household. By the end of 1843, Lovelace began taking a variety of medicines. Although she had many other projects in mind, ill health, mind-clouding medication, lack of focus, and inadequate intellectual support from those close to her undermined her plans.

In the absence of other projects, Lovelace turned her attention to the mathematics of gambling on horses, pawning her jewels and going into debt to finance the habit. As her health worsened, she indulged more often in wine; at one point she proposed writing an analysis of the effects of wine and opium, based on personal experience. She kept up close and flirtatious friendships with a number of men, and at her death her husband burned a hundred of her letters.

ADA LOVELACE BY MARGARET SARAH CARPENTER

By early 1852, Lovelace began to suffer from severe abdominal pains. Opium and mathematics provided her only comfort. Her husband William King wrote of her, "Her mind was invigorated by the society of the intellectual men whom she entertained as guests. . . . She mastered the mathematical side of a question in all its minuteness . . . her power of generalisation was indeed most remarkable, coupled as it was with that of minute and intricate analysis." But in Ada Lovelace's final months, her daughter Annabella and mother Lady Byron hovered over her, denying admission to other visitors. They persuaded Lovelace to undergo a religious revival and to repent of her past transgressions.

In November, still only thirty-six years old, Ada Augusta Byron, Countess of Lovelace, died of uterine cancer. One hundred twenty-seven years later, the U.S. Department of Defense named a new computer language "Ada" in her honor.

"The Enchantress of Numbers."

Timeline | 1815-1910

Ada Byron born | 1815

Birth of Florence Nightingale | 1820

OLIVER TWIST

ETHER

Nightingale nurses her family during | 1837
influenza epidemic

1838 | Dickens publishes Oliver Twist

Semmelweis shows hand-washing | 1847
prevents deaths in childbirth

1846 | First use of ether for surgical anesthesia

1847 | Meets Sidney Herbert in Rome

1853 | Superintendent of Nursing at Institution
for the Care of Sick Gentlewomen

John Snow shows that cholera is spread | 1854
through contaminated water

1854 | Sails to Crimea

1856 | Returns to England

Notes on Nursing | 1859

Nightingale School for Nurses opens | 1860

1859 | Charles Darwin publishes
Origin of Species

1868 | Royal Sanitary
Commission
begins work

Pasteur develops rabies vaccine | 1880

Clara Barton founds American | 1881
Red Cross

DARWIN CARICATURE

CLARA BARTON
STAMP

Death of Florence Nightingale at age 90 | 1910

6 | *Health Care Researcher and Statistician*

Florence Nightingale

1820-1910 | *England*

Most people, when they think of Florence Nightingale, do not associate her with mathematics. What comes to mind instead is the iconic image of the Lady with the Lamp, a stately, compassionate figure moving quietly among the beds of English soldiers wounded in the Crimean War. Yet Nightingale's first biographer called his book *Passionate Statistician*. Nightingale's pioneering use of statistics to lay the foundation of evidence-based health care turned out to be just as fundamental as her campaign to make nursing an independent health profession.

Born in Florence, Italy, Nightingale was raised in England in a wealthy family that wished her only to marry well and take her place in society. Although he foresaw for his daughters no profession beyond motherhood, William Nightingale, Florence's father, valued education. Once his daughters surpassed what a governess could teach them, he taught them himself, instructing them in Latin, Greek, French, and Italian; the rudiments of chemistry, geography, and physics; elementary mathematics; and history. Florence often rose at three in the morning to work on her Greek, and she clearly outshone her less scholarly sister Parthenope.

STATUE OF FLORENCE NIGHTINGALE

During her mid-teens, Florence became increasingly aware of the poverty and illness among the villagers near her father's estates. Along with her mother or an aunt, she paid sick visits, bringing medicine and blankets, sitting by bedsides, and keeping case notes on villagers beset by long illnesses. In January 1837, when a bout of influenza laid almost the entire Nightingale household low, Florence acted as "nurse, governess, assistant curate and doctor" until her family recovered. At the end of the influenza epidemic, seventeen-year-old Florence Nightingale had a religious experience in which, as she wrote, "God spoke to me and called me to his service." Unfortunately, nursing, the form of service that attracted her, was socially unacceptable to her family.

To Florence's mother Fanny, what was most important was the family's position in society. As for Florence's older sister Parthenope, she tended to fall into hysterics whenever her younger sister took a step toward independence. William Nightingale tended to withdraw from family conflict without taking sides. As a dutiful daughter with strong religious sensibilities, Florence Nightingale found herself torn between family duty and her sense of a higher calling. In an unfinished novel, *Cassandra*, Nightingale later expressed her frustration: "Why has woman passion, intellect, moral activity — these three — and a place in society where no one of the three can be exercised?"

Throughout her twenties, Florence Nightingale lived the life expected of a woman of her class, despite chafing at the restrictions put upon her. She traveled with her family through Europe, keeping statistics on the journey, noting times and distances as well as laws and customs. Back in England she acquired two suitors. For years, God did not speak to her again, and Nightingale became convinced of her own unworthiness. She fell more frequently into the near trances she called her "vice of dreaming."

SIDNEY HERBERT

Certain that marriage and motherhood could never satisfy her, Nightingale made a plan: she would work in a hospital and learn the basics of nursing. Her family reacted with horror. Hospitals were filthy, smelly places, and nurses were often drunken and coarse. Surgeons expected the nurses' sexual favors on demand. Nightingale's family forbade her to set out, and rather than defy them, she fell into a depression. "I shall never do anything," she wrote a friend, "and am worse than dust and nothing . . . Oh for some strong thing to sweep this loathsome life into the past."

In 1847, a middle-aged couple named the Bracebridges rescued Nightingale by taking her to Rome. There she met Sidney Herbert, the former and future Secretary of State for War, in an encounter that proved to be one of the most important of her life. It was through Herbert's intervention that she later went to the Crimea, and through his efforts that many of her later sanitary reforms became law.

Home once more, bored and feeling useless, Nightingale set herself to learn everything she could about hospitals. She gathered reports about the sick from all over Europe, collated and analyzed them. To the intense disappointment of her family, she finally rejected her suitor, the poet, politician, and literary patron Richard Monckton Milnes. She wrote, "I have a moral and active nature which requires satisfaction . . . I could not satisfy this nature by spending a life with him in making society and arranging domestic things . . . Voluntarily to put it out of my power ever to be able to seize the chance of forming for myself a true and rich life would seem to me like suicide." Yet she desperately missed Milnes, his sympathy and his intelligence.

Once again, Florence Nightingale hovered on the edge of a breakdown, and once again the Bracebridges rescued her. This time they took her to Egypt, where God spoke to her again and "asked me would I do well for Him alone without the reputation." She answered yes. She fell ill in Athens, but when she recovered, the Bracebridges took her to Germany, where together they spent a fortnight at Kaiserswerth, an institution Nightingale had long yearned to visit. Founded by a Lutheran pastor, Kaiserswerth combined an orphanage, a penitentiary, and a hospital, and it offered training to women who wished to work with the less fortunate. Inspired, Nightingale wrote and published a pamphlet on the Institution's work.

But once again, when she returned home, Nightingale fell into depression. Her family opposed her ambitions, and she thought of death with longing. "In my thirty-first year I see nothing desirable but death. . . . Why, oh my God, can I not be satisfied with the life that satisfies so many people?"

> *"I have a moral and active nature which requires satisfaction."*

In desperation, Florence Nightingale finally stood up for herself. Her sister Parthenope was supposed to take a three-month cure at Carlsbad. During that time, Florence announced, she would go to Kaiserswerth for nurse training. Frightful arguments followed. Parthenope had hysterics. Florence fainted. But she left for Kaiserswerth the next day.

Life at Kaiserswerth was Spartan and rigorous, yet joyful. The trainees rose before dawn, ate gruel, broth, and vegetables, and worked all day. The hospital was filthy and the training meager, but the entire institution was filled with a spirit of dedication. Nightingale wrote to her sister, "This is Life. Now I know what it is to live and to love life." Her mother and sister kept her whereabouts quiet, as if it were cause for shame. Three months later Nightingale was home and once more trapped in her family role. She nursed her father and a dying great-aunt, but nothing more.

Then, in 1853, Florence Nightingale finally had her chance. A committee of charitable London ladies had decided to create an Institution for the Care of Sick Gentlewomen, and they needed a Superintendent of Nursing. A friend put Nightingale's name forward, and she was accepted. Threats, hysterics, and fainting fits did not deter her. In the end, William Nightingale supported his

MATHEMATICS

FLORENCE NIGHTINGALE

The **Crimean War** began when the Ottoman Empire declared war on Russia in October 1853. The immediate cause was a dispute over who should oversee the rights of Christians in the Holy Land, but a deeper cause was Russia's desire to control the Black Sea and encroach upon lands of the weakening Ottoman Empire. Britain, France, and Sardinia joined the war on the Ottoman side, and after fierce fighting, took the Russian naval base at Sevastopol. Russia sued for peace in March, 1856. The war was the first to be well documented by journalists and photographers, and in Britain it led to demands for modernizing armies and medical care.

daughter's move, giving her an allowance of five hundred pounds a year, equivalent to about $50,000 today.

For fourteen months, Nightingale worked as she had never worked before. She furnished the house at One Harley Street for patient comfort, installed innovations like bells to call for help, recruited nurses, insisted that women of all religions be admitted, bought vegetables in Covent Garden, negotiated with committees, and rubbed patients' feet at night. Her patients loved her, but in the end the little institution at Harley Street could not contain all her enthusiasm. She took a leave of absence to nurse victims of a cholera epidemic at Middlesex Hospital, where her patients included poor prostitutes and drunkards. Then she announced her intention to seek the post of Superintendent of Nurses at King's College Hospital, where she could reorganize the nurse training program.

Nightingale's plans changed in March 1854, when France and England declared war on Russia, and the Crimean War began. Thousands of British soldiers shipped out to the shores of the Black Sea to support their besieged Turkish allies. Cholera broke out among the crowded troops, and following the bloody battle of Alma, outraged letters from a *London Times* correspondent exposed the Army's disastrously inadequate care for sick and wounded soldiers. Ashamed, *Times* readers immediately began to raise funds, and in mid-October, Florence Nightingale's friend Sidney Herbert, now once again Secretary of State for War, asked her to lead a team of nurses to the war zone.

Nightingale did not hesitate. On the 21st of October, she set sail with a purse full of *Times* donations and with thirty-eight women, including Roman Catholic nuns and her own Aunt Mai. Sidney Herbert had assured her that medical stores had been sent ahead "in profusion," but Nightingale spent some of the *Times* fund on supplies of her own, including portable stoves. Her corps of nurses sailed through a severe gale before arriving at the hospital of Scutari, across the sea from the Crimean peninsula, where the sick and wounded men were housed in an old barracks. There were no tables, nothing to cook with,

HOSPITAL AT SCUTARI, LITHOGRAPH

and a water allowance of only one pint per man per day. Rats and damp abounded. The privies were blocked, and sewage overflowed. Sidney Herbert's profusion of medical supplies had never arrived.

Nightingale threw herself into all of it. She took over the kitchens, organized proper food, trained and ruled her nurses, and fought with the purveyor to release the stores Herbert had sent. She rented a Turkish house, had boilers installed, and hired soldiers' wives to wash the hospital linens. Gradually conditions improved. During Nightingale's first winter at Scutari, more than 4,000 soldiers died there, mostly of fever; but once Britain sent out a Sanitary Commission to clean out the sewers and improve ventilation, death rates eventually dropped from a peak of over fifty percent of admissions to a more usual ten percent and then a creditable two percent. Better weather and a drop in overcrowding helped.

With Scutari in good condition, Nightingale arranged an inspection tour of hospitals across the sea on the Crimean peninsula itself. She visited three hospitals, and soldiers in the trenches at Sevastopol cheered her, but two weeks after her arrival, Nightingale fell dangerously ill with "Crimean fever," most probably brucellosis. For nine days she hovered near death. Then, emaciated, weak, with her head shaved and her voice a whisper, Nightingale was shipped back to Scutari. There she recovered gradually, spending much of her time writing letters and devoting herself to the soldiers' moral betterment by providing them a library, schoolmasters for the illiterate, and opportunities to send money home rather than spend it on drink. She remained too weak to resume her nursing duties.

Brucellosis, or undulant fever, is a bacterial infection first described during the Crimean War. The source is unpasteurized milk, soft cheese, or undercooked meat from infected animals, often goats or cows. Symptoms of the acute illness include waves of fever and intense sweating, along with joint and muscle pain. Without antibiotics, most patients recover initially, but they may suffer all their lives from chronically recurring symptoms such as headache, joint pains, sweats, chronic fatigue, and depression. One common late symptom, shared by Florence Nightingale, is spondylitis, severe pain from inflammation of the vertebral bones in the back.

In 1856, only twenty-one months after her arrival, the war ended, and Nightingale returned to England clothed in almost saint-like status. Portraits had been painted of her; poems had been written. Despite her admirers, Nightingale managed to slip into the country quietly, take a train, and walk across a field to surprise her family. She avoided a fuss, but the next day the church bells in her village rang wildly.

> *"I wish we had her at the War Office."*
> – Queen Victoria

Memories of emaciated men with open sores dying in hordes in Scutari's first winter preyed on Nightingale's mind, and she could not rest until she put forward her ideas about how to reform the Army Medical Department. Her chance came when Queen Victoria invited her to a series of informal conversations in Scotland. Both the Queen and Prince Albert were impressed with her quiet certainty. "I wish we had her at the War Office," Victoria wrote, and she established a Royal Commission to investigate further.

Being a woman, Nightingale was not appointed to the Commission. Instead, she worked tirelessly behind the scenes, first negotiating with the new Secretary of State for War to get seats on the Commission for her allies, including her friend Sidney Herbert, who was appointed chair. It took six long months before the Commission met, but Nightingale used that time to amass her evidence. She began with a careful investigation of the causes of death during the Crimean War.

Nightingale's main tool for changing minds was going to be carefully written reports and proposals based on statistical analysis. "To understand God's thoughts," she wrote, "we must understand statistics, for these are the workings of his purpose." She refined her statistical approach by corresponding with the Belgian social statistician Adolphe Quetelet. Then, working with William Farr, a physician and statistician, she combed through official records and created charts, tables, and graphs. One of her first discoveries was that the initial death rate at Scutari, even after she had brought in food and clean laundry, had been much greater than at front line hospitals where the shortage of supplies was, if anything, worse. The difference, Nightingale realized, was that Scutari had been built over a cesspool, so that raw sewage leaked into the water supply. Rigorous examination of evidence had convinced her: for the rest of her life, Florence Nightingale focused upon sanitation above all in matters of public health.

To demonstrate that the vast majority of deaths during the Crimean War had resulted from disease rather than bullets, Nightingale invented a new way of presenting data. Her polar area diagram was a refinement of the familiar pie chart, one that could show in one image three attributes, such as time, cause of death, and number of deaths. Piled up together, these charts made a collection she called a "coxcomb." Though Farr helped her prepare the charts, he was skeptical. Statistics, he

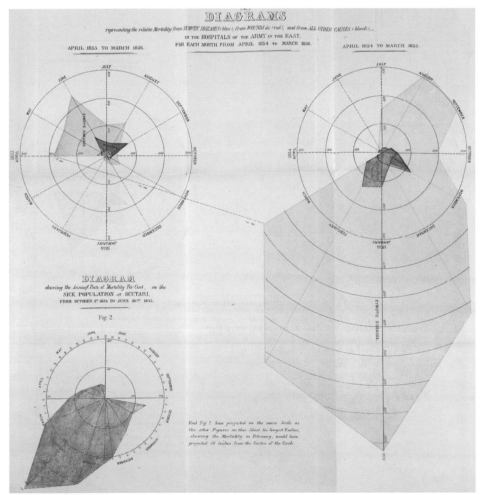

NIGHTINGALE'S POLAR DIAGRAMS (COXCOMBS), COURTESY OF RONALD SMELTZER

said, should be dry, the dryer the better. But Nightingale believed that her coxcombs could help those who were not mathematically minded comprehend the facts.

Nightingale met constantly with the reformist commissioners, briefing them and preparing them for taking testimony. Living in the Burlington Hotel, close to where the Commission met, Nightingale worked herself into a state of collapse, falling so ill that her family feared for her survival. But her efforts bore fruit. Although her own direct written testimony took up only thirty pages, the Commission's 600-page report relied heavily on her prepared evidence. The recommendations for reform came straight from her. They included proposals for a Statistical Corps in the Army Medical Department, for a special Army medical school, for a male and female nursing corps, and for sanitation, ventilation, food and wholesome activities for soldiers in the barracks. Even after the Commission's report was issued, Nightingale continued to coax, cajole, and argue until much of it was adopted.

> *"To understand God's thoughts, we must understand statistics."*

Next Nightingale turned her analysis to the welfare of the Army in India, then to health care data for India in general, and then to hospitals in Britain. She struggled to convince officials that statistics provide the best tool for guiding decisions. She created a standard statistical form by which hospitals could collect data, and its use was approved at the 1860 International Statistical Conference. However, a few years later, the London hospitals abandoned Nightingale's form as "too costly and time consuming."

Nightingale never fully recovered from the breakdown in her health that befell her during the Commission's work. From 1857 on, she lived as an invalid, housebound and often bedridden. Her symptoms included palpitations, nausea, depression, insomnia, weakness, and irritability. Many of these symptoms were non-specific, and doctors of the day generally attributed them to stress and overwork, while some later writers considered her a malingerer, using her illness to keep her family and unwanted visitors from impinging on her time. But in 1861, Nightingale began to suffer bouts of extreme back pain consistent with spondylitis, an inflammation of the spine characteristic of chronic brucellosis. Most likely, her lifelong illness was a chronic recurrence of her "Crimean fever."

Bedridden or not, Nightingale maintained a pace of work that would overwhelm most people. She wrote numerous reports, pamphlets, books, and at least 14,000 letters in her lifetime. Sleeping little and limiting her visitors to scheduled half-hour appointments, she dashed off reports, complaints, appeals, and works of religious philosophy. Her conviction that she might soon die gave her work urgency. A persuasive correspondent and relentless organizer, she designed hospitals, wrote a nursing text, and oversaw the founding of the Nightingale School for nurse training at St. Thomas' Hospital.

SIX VICTORIAN TOWERS OF ST. THOMAS' HOSPITAL

Florence Nightingale was the first woman to be elected a Fellow of the Royal Statistical Society and the first to receive the Order of Merit, Britain's highest civilian honor. But her most important honors were the reforms she instituted, including improved hospital design, better health for British soldiers, better sanitation in homes and hospitals, adequate hunger relief in India, and the creation of the Army Medical Department's Statistical Branch. Besides these social reforms, Nightingale truly established nursing as an independent profession whose practitioners could rise to the top and rule their own working lives. By the time she died peacefully at age ninety, much of the frantic work of her middle years had come to fruition.

Florence Nightingale holds a unique place among the women in this book. None of them better expressed the pain of being a gifted female in a society that made no place for one. None of them fought harder or longer against their own families to achieve the freedom they needed to do their work. Only Marie Curie was as revered as Florence Nightingale: the press presented both of them as ideal feminine figures, selfless and devoted. But although Florence Nightingale served for a few months as a good and caring nurse, her true talents lay in politics and administration, and her power lay in her unyielding will and her sharp analytical mind. Although she is justly remembered as the founder of modern nursing, her contributions to the foundations of scientific, evidence-based health care were just as fundamental and just as profound.

Timeline | 1842–1910

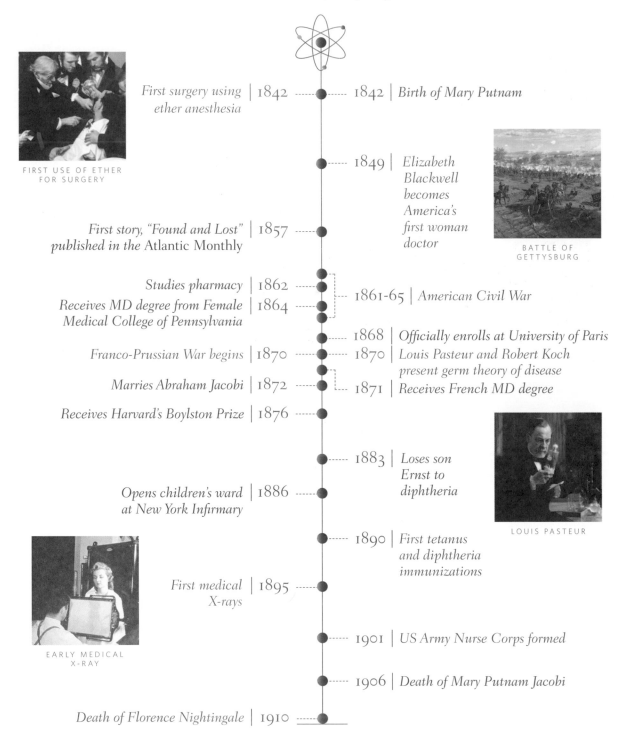

First surgery using | 1842 ⎯⎯ 1842 | Birth of Mary Putnam
ether anesthesia

FIRST USE OF ETHER
FOR SURGERY

⎯⎯ 1849 | Elizabeth
Blackwell
becomes
America's
first woman
doctor

First story, "Found and Lost" | 1857 ⎯⎯
published in the Atlantic Monthly

BATTLE OF
GETTYSBURG

Studies pharmacy | 1862 ⎯⎯
Receives MD degree from Female | 1864 ⎯⎯   1861–65 | American Civil War
Medical College of Pennsylvania

⎯⎯ 1868 | Officially enrolls at University of Paris
Franco-Prussian War begins | 1870 ⎯⎯ 1870 | Louis Pasteur and Robert Koch
present germ theory of disease
Marries Abraham Jacobi | 1872 ⎯⎯ 1871 | Receives French MD degree

Receives Harvard's Boylston Prize | 1876 ⎯⎯

1883 | Loses son
Ernst to
diphtheria

Opens children's ward | 1886 ⎯⎯
at New York Infirmary

LOUIS PASTEUR

1890 | First tetanus
and diphtheria
immunizations

First medical | 1895 ⎯⎯
X-rays

EARLY MEDICAL
X-RAY

1901 | US Army Nurse Corps formed

1906 | Death of Mary Putnam Jacobi

Death of Florence Nightingale | 1910 ⎯⎯

7 | *Through a Different Door*

Mary Putnam Jacobi

1842-1906 | *United States*

Precocious and determined, Mary Corinna Putnam, called Minnie by her family, yearned to make her mark in the world. At age ten, she wrote in her journal, "Vague longings beset me. I imagine great things and glorious deeds; but ah! The vision passes like a fleeting dream and the muddy reality is left behind. I would be great. I would do deeds . . ."

Born in London on August 31, 1842, Minnie Putnam was the eldest child of the publisher George Putnam and his young French wife Victorine. Early in Minnie's childhood, the family moved to Staten Island to live among country meadows swept by sea breezes. Victorine Putnam taught the children French, English, arithmetic and music. The rest of the time, Minnie ran free, imitating her brothers' headstands or wanting to dissect a dead rat. When she got too wild, she was confined to her room, where she stood on the balcony watching ships pass the island. One day Minnie swam out too far from the beach and had to be rescued by a workman; she was astonished the next day when her father gave the rescuer a silver watch.

Soon after Minnie wrote of her vague longings for glory, the family moved to New York City, then to Yonkers. By that time there were seven children. A tutor led the older children in Latin exercises, and Minnie organized a debating club among the young people of the neighborhood. She was a scholarly girl,

> *"I imagine great things and glorious deeds."*

but no matter how much she loved reading and winning debates, she dreaded leaving outdoor life and childhood behind. To her journal she confided, "The stiff hedge of decorum binds me in. I am expected to cut off my childish things, to become a woman, while my heart is yet young, and why? Because I have approached my twelfth birthday."

In her teens, Minnie attended school for the first time—a progressive girls' school— and found it boring. To challenge herself, she wrote stories. At age fifteen she earned eighteen dollars for her first publication, a story in the *Atlantic Monthly* called "Found and Lost." Her father counted the earnings out into Minnie's hand in pieces of gold.

Struggling over how to reconcile her desire for glory with the need for decorum, Minnie sought the answer in religion. Her grandmother Putnam encouraged her to think about salvation, so Minnie focused on suppressing her pride and sinfulness. She became a Baptist and wrote long letters analyzing her character flaws. Then, a few years later, her faith took a blow when her church's charismatic young minister drowned at age twenty-five. Minnie's questions became too challenging for her grandmother's Bible class, and at age twenty-one she broke away from the church.

After leaving school, Mary Putnam, as she now called herself, took private lessons in Greek, tutored her younger siblings, and taught classes in a girls' school. But she wanted more, and at the age of twenty, she entered the New York College of Pharmacy. With the help of private lessons in science, she earned her degree the next year.

Next Putnam set her sights on medical school. This was one step too far for her doting father, who offered her $250 a year to postpone her studies and help her mother with the younger children—now up to thirteen in all—instead. Circumstance intervened. The Civil War was underway, and Mary's brother Haven, stationed with the 176th New York regiment in New Orleans, came down with a fever, most likely malaria. Mary sailed to New Orleans to nurse him. Her semi-military post required her to take an oath to perform all the duties of a "true and loyal citizen;" in later years she acidly pointed out that these included the duty to vote, which would not be allowed to women for nearly seventy more years.

With her brother safe, Putnam returned and enrolled in the Female Medical College of Pennsylvania, the first medical school for American women. Her worried father wrote to her,

> *Now Minnie, you know very well that I am proud of your abilities and am willing that you should apply them even to the repulsive pursuit . . . of Medical Science. But don't let yourself be absorbed and gobbled up in that branch of the animal kingdom ordinarily called strong minded women. **Don't** let them intensify your self-will and independence for they are strong enough already."*

Her mother, on the other hand, warned her not to let her hat be untidy—"These things so stamp a woman's character."

After a brief course of study, Mary Putnam received her medical degree in the spring of 1864. She went to work, first in a hospital in Philadelphia and another in Boston, but then returned home to study more chemistry while working in the East Side. Her father dispatched one of her brothers to sit in on the chemistry classes so Mary would not be the sole pupil of her male instructor.

Then another family member fell ill. Mary's sister Edith, teaching freed slaves in Port Royal, South Carolina, came down with typhoid fever. Mary rushed south to nurse her, and Edith, though she lost all her hair, gradually recovered.

Returning to New York, Mary Putnam became engaged to her chemistry tutor, Ferdinand Mayer, a penniless Jewish immigrant ten years her senior. Her family was shocked but did not forbid the marriage. But Putnam herself soon wavered, writing to her father, "I am not sure that his intellect or character are as strong as mine." Her father encouraged her to break off the engagement at once.

Still restless, and dissatisfied with her education, Mary Putnam wanted to reach further. She wanted to go to Paris, to study with the most eminent physicians of the day. First, though, she had to earn some money. She moved to New Orleans to tutor a young boy for admission to West Point. For extra money, she also wrote a series of character sketches for the Sunday edition of the New Orleans *Times*. Between the two jobs, she saved enough to set sail for France in September 1866, just after she turned twenty-four.

MARY PUTNAM JACOBI AS A YOUNG WOMAN, FROM THE LIBRARY OF CONGRESS.

Doors did not open easily to a young American woman wanting to study medicine in Paris. With the help of her mentor Dr. Edith Blackwell, Putnam found lodging in a fifth floor room in the Latin Quarter. "Towers of Notre Dame loom up grandly through the slight silvery mist like a dream," she wrote. She immersed herself in the study of French and of Paris.

Refused admission to the University of Paris medical school, Putnam nevertheless gained permission to follow general hospital clinics and clinics for nervous diseases. She also attended lectures at the museum of the *Jardin des Plantes*, or botanical gardens. Gradually she pieced together a first-class education for herself. She spent no time on frivolity. For one thing, she had no illusions of being pretty. With severe objectivity, she described herself:

Hands and feet and head all too large for the height . . . Eyes large, well set, dark and bright, but without enough eyelashes and frequently reddened at the lids . . . Complexion . . . too thick and with brown and sallow tints . . . Whole face square and massive, with square chin and black level eyebrows.

She was content with her appearance, she wrote home, because a pretty woman would never be allowed to attend the hospitals.

Money was tight. Whenever she could, Putnam wrote articles on French affairs for the *New York Evening Post*. She also undertook a series of letters from Paris to *The Medical Record*, sharing medical and surgical advances she observed. A couple of hours of tutoring a night also supplemented her income. Despite these efforts, Putnam had no extra money for finery, a fact that encouraged her to spend her time studying or working. "You see at the hospitals you are not expected to wear anything nice, and when I get out of clothes, I stop visiting and only go the to the hospitals." When her father sent her money for a new dress, she asked if she might spend it on a microscope instead.

Over time, Putnam worked her way into more lectures and clinics, acting as a student or intern, writing up cases and following patients. She gained access to the medical library and to a practical course in anatomy. She wrote, "I have exactly father's temperament for working which does not tire me the least in the world."

"How few people . . . really work hard and love their work!"

Still, the Paris School of Medicine faculty refused to admit her as a regular student. Finally they settled on a compromise, which allowed Mary Putnam to enter by a side door and take her seat in a reserved place beside the professor. She had finally found her separate door into the medical profession. She reported that

"The students, who all know me by sight, do not lift an eyebrow at my appearance, taking it as a matter of course, —I pull out my inkstand and take my notes, and feel as much at home as if I had been there all my life."

In June 1868, with the opposition worn out, Putnam was officially inscribed as a student in the school. One week later, along with two male students, she took the first of a series of key examinations. One of the young men was so intimidated by the examiners that he bolted from the room, while the second bumbled through, but Putnam passed with high marks: *très satisfait*. So things continued for the next three years, despite the school closing once for a student protest and once for the outbreak of the Franco-Prussian war. Putnam loved it. When she compared immersion in technical studies to eating arsenic, she meant it as praise. "Once begun you must go on, and at a continually increasing dose. I am really astonished to find how this absorption grows upon me." She was equally astonished by "how few people, even in a great centre like this, really work hard, and love their work; how many merely use it as a make-shift for money or reputation or a lazy *passé-temps!*"

Beginning in October 1869, Putnam boarded with the family of the geographer and anarchist, Élisée Reclus. Around the Reclus family table, Putnam was able to participate in the kinds of intellectual and political discussion she remembered from her own family. Socialists who were also deeply interested in women's rights, the Reclus became Putnam's closest friends in France.

In the midst of her medical studies, Putnam continued to write and publish. "A Sermon in Notre Dame," a story set during a cholera epidemic and published in the *Atlantic Monthly* in 1868, proclaims the failure of religion and the importance of public action to defend public health. In 1871, during the siege of Paris, she wrote an article about the creation of the French Republic.

During the Siege of Paris, Putnam continued her studies as long as possible. When the city was bombed, she took refuge in the Pantheon. Only when the medical school closed did she travel briefly to London. As soon as the school reopened, she returned and passed her fifth and final exam. Only her doctoral thesis stood between her and graduation. Defending her thesis on "Neutral Fat and Fatty Acids" in front of a three hundred spectators, she received a bronze medal and the highest grade, *Extrèmement satisfait.*

Armed with her French degree, Putnam returned to America in September 1871. She took a position as professor of *materia medica* and therapeutics—chemistry and pharmacology—at the Women's Medical College of the New York Infirmary, where she cared for patients, carried out research, and taught. Her lofty goal was "the creation of a scientific spirit (which at present does not exist), among women medical students." In 1872 she organized the Association for the Advancement of the Medical Education of Women, and she served as its president from 1874 to 1903. Also in 1872, the New York

The **Franco-Prussian War** *(July 1870 – May 1871) between the Northern German Confederation and Second Empire France grew out of a dispute over the Spanish succession. When France voted for war, German armies rapidly invaded, taking advantage of railroads, superior manpower, and artillery. Germany defeated the French army and captured Emperor Napoleon III at Sedan. Without its emperor, France declared the Third Republic on September 4, 1870, but the German advance continued, and following the* **Siege of Paris***, the capital fell on January 28, 1871.*

In March, 1871, the working people of Paris, led by socialists, seized power and formed the revolutionary **Paris Commune***. The Commune lasted only two months before the regular French army suppressed it in a week of bloody street battles.*

In the aftermath of the war, the German states united under Wilhelm I, and Germany became Europe's dominant power.

Academy of Medicine, chaired by Dr. Abraham Jacobi, made Mary Putnam a member.

The next year, Abraham Jacobi and Mary Putnam married. Considered the father of American pediatrics, Jacobi was one of the most prominent physicians of the day. He was also a Jewish immigrant and a reformer, a founder both of the *American Journal of Obstetrics* and the American Communist Party. A few years earlier, Putnam had written home,

ABRAHAM JACOBI

> *I have no particular desire to marry at any time; nevertheless, if at home, I should ever come across a physician, intelligent, refined, more enthusiastic for his science than me, but who would like me, and for whom I should entertain about the same feeling that I have for Haven [her brother], I think I would marry such a person if he asked me, and would leave me full liberty to exercise my profession.*

Apparently Jacobi, who combined excellence in medicine with a social sensibility reminiscent of the Reclus family, met Putnam's criteria. Together the couple lost one child in infancy and then had a son and daughter. Mary Putnam Jacobi continued to exercise her profession, teaching, seeing patients, and doing research.

In 1875, Putnam Jacobi turned to research to refute a paper published by Dr. Edward C. Clarke. Titled "Sex in Education; or, A Fair Chance for the Girls," Clarke's paper suggested that women's

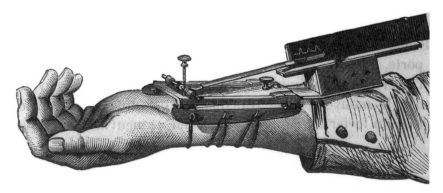

SPHYGMOGRAPH FOR MEASURING STRENGTH OF THE PULSE

weakness, and in particular the rigors of their monthly cycle, made them ill-suited to the expanded role they were seeking in society and the professions. Mary Putnam Jacobi responded with a wealth of research data, including tables and statistics showing that women's pulse, blood pressure, and temperature remained stable throughout their menstrual cycles. So that her paper would not be dismissed out of hand as the work of a disgruntled woman, Putnam Jacobi submitted it anonymously under the motto, "*Veritas poemate verior*," – "a truth truer than a poem." Despite stirring up controversy, the essay, entitled "The Question of Rest for Women during Menstruation," was awarded Harvard's prestigious Boylston Medical Prize in 1876. The award was all the more significant because the medical school had just voted to reject a donation of $10,000, worth about $220,000 in 2014 dollars, rather than start admitting women.

For sixteen years, Putnam Jacobi gave five lectures a week on *materia medica* at the Women's Medical College. Despite her high hopes, her students usually disappointed her: she found them ill-prepared and less devoted to study than she had been. Moreover, she had a difference of philosophy with Dr. Blackwell, the founder of the College. Elizabeth Blackwell held that women physicians were different from men, and as such needed a different preparation. Women, she argued, were more spiritually attuned than their male counterparts. Disease, she believed, grew from moral impurity, and medicine itself was at heart a moral calling that should focus on moral and social reform. Mary Putnam Jacobi, by contrast, insisted on a scientific approach and held that, in order to compete in the cozy world of male practitioners, women physicians needed to be rigorously prepared in the sciences. In 1888, these differences led Putnam Jacobi to resign her teaching post. Meanwhile, in 1882, she joined the faculty of the New York Post-Graduate Medical School as clinical lecturer on the diseases of children—the first appointment of an American woman to teach in a co-educational medical school.

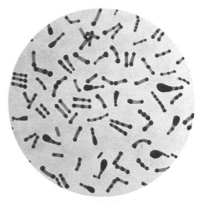

DIPHTHERIA

*The symptoms of **diphtheria** include fever, sore throat, swollen lymph nodes, and difficulty breathing. The cause is a club-shaped bacterium called Corynebacterium diphtheria. The bacterium secretes a toxin that invades cells in the mucous membranes of the mouth and throat, causing a grayish, firm membrane to coat the tonsils and throat. The membrane may obstruct the airway or extend down the trachea into the bronchi. In five to ten percent of cases, death comes, usually by choking or cardiac failure.*

In 1883, the same year that Ernst Jacobi died of diphtheria, Edwin Klebs identified the bacterium that caused it. In 1891, the first person was treated with diphtheria antitoxin isolated from the blood of horses that had been immunized with small doses of diphtheria toxin. By the 1920's, a heat-inactivated toxin called a toxoid was used as a vaccine, allowing people to build their own immunity against the disease. Diphtheria toxoid is now part of the DPT injections given to young children. As a result, diphtheria has been virtually eliminated in the US, although outbreaks continue in the rest of the world whenever vaccination rates fall.

In 1883, after a happy decade of marriage, research, and practice, Abraham and Mary Putnam Jacobi lost their son Ernst to diphtheria. The loss was made more bitter by the fact that Abraham Jacobi, although he rejected the emerging germ theory of disease, was the leading American expert on diphtheria at the time, often performing tracheostomies as a last desperate measure to save a patient.

Despite her sorrow and her husband's profound distress, Putnam Jacobi continued to branch out in her practice and research. In 1886, she opened a children's ward at the New York Infirmary. She also became one of the earliest medical researchers to investigate pediatric neurology. Through dissection, she located the lesion of polio in the motor neurons of the spinal cord, a discovery which helped lead to the development of the polio vaccine seventy-five years later. She wrote over one hundred scientific articles and nine books. In one book, *Physiological Notes and Primary Education and the Study of Language,* she used experiment and observation,

ERNST JACOBI, AGE 3

ANATOMY LECTURE HALL AT NY MEDICAL COLLEGE FOR WOMEN,
WHERE MARY PUTNAM JACOBI TAUGHT

statistics and neurology, to examine the question of how children acquire language and how they might best learn. In another, *Common Sense Applied to Woman Suffrage*, she drew on history, philosophy, and statistics to argue that the time to give women the vote had arrived.

Throughout the late 1800s, Mary Putnam Jacobi was widely recognized as the leading woman physician of her day, and indeed as one of the leading American physicians of either sex. Her capacity for work continued to be immense until 1900, when the occasional headaches and nausea she had been suffering for four years became severe. She diagnosed a brain tumor, and in 1903 she began a final paper: "Description of the Early Symptoms of the Meningeal Tumor Compressing the Cerebellum. From Which the Writer Died. Written by Herself."

Mary Putnam Jacobi died on June 10, 1906 at the age of 63. Through her teach-

SIR WILLIAM OSLER C1912

ing, her example, and her writing, she had helped establish the scientific basis of American medicine. Besides her direct contributions to neurology, pediatrics and women's medicine, her example and the high standards she advocated for women's medical education had cleared the way for other women to follow. She had built institutions and established precedents. In his eulogy, Dr. William Osler opined that the fact that "almost everywhere the door is now open" to women physicians was largely due to the quality of Putnam Jacobi's scientific contributions.

> *"Almost everywhere the door is now open."*
>
> – William Osler, MD

Timeline | 1848-1895

Marx publishes | 1848
Communist
Manifesto

KARL_MARX

1850 | *Birth of*
Sofia Korvin-
Kirakovskaya,
later Kovalevskaya

1859 | *Darwin's* Origin of Species *published*

Tsar Alexander II | 1861
frees the serfs.
American Civil
War begins

1864 | *Teaches*
herself
trigonometry

FIRST IMPRESSIONIST
EXHIBITION

Marries; leaves Russia to study | 1869
mathematics in Germany

1871 | *Paris Commune*

Receives doctorate in mathematics | 1874

1874 | *First Impressionist*
Exhibition in Paris

Bell invents | 1876
the telephone

1875 | *Returns to Russia*

BELL TELEPHONE

1883 | *Lectures in*
Stockholm

Seurat finishes A | 1886
Sunday Afternoon at
La Grande Jatte

1888 | *Wins mathematics prize*
from French Academy of Sciences

Publishes The | 1890
Nihilist Girl

1891 | *Death of Sofia Kovalevskaya*

SEURAT'S SUNDAY AT
LA GRANDE JATTE

Roentgen | 1895
discovers
X-rays

8 | *The Exalted and Mysterious Science*

Sophie Kovalevskaya

1850-1891 | *Russia*

SOPHIE KOVALEVSKAYA.

An eleven-year-old girl stood in her bedroom and gazed at the walls, stirred by a strange excitement. It was 1861, and her father, a Russian general and member of the minor nobility, had settled his family in Palabino, his estate outside of Moscow. Lacking wall-paper, the family had papered the walls of Sophie's room with pages from the gener-al's old calculus lecture notes. Sophie stared at the elegant symbols and swirling S's—integration signs, though she did not recognize them at the time. They reminded her of her uncle Pyotr, who talked about math in a way that called forth in Sophie, as she later wrote, "a reverence for mathematics as an exalted and mysterious science."

Sofia Korvin-Krukovskaya, as she was then known, was the middle child, neither as pretty as her beloved older sister Anna nor as treasured as the longed-for heir, her younger brother Fedya. Sophie attributed her lifelong shyness to the fact that she was her parents' least favorite child. Only in mathematics did Sophie really step out of Anna's shadow. She wrote later that while working with her tutor, "I began to feel an attrac-tion for my mathematics so intense that I started to neglect my other studies." When Sophie's father, "who had a horror of learned women," tried to put a stop to her mathematics les-sons, Sophie smuggled in an algebra textbook to read under the covers at night.

Without the knowledge of their father the general, Sophie's sister Anna was also trying her hand at unladylike behavior. In secret, she wrote short stories, and then a novel. Even more scandalously, she earned money by doing so. When a servant mistakenly brought the general a letter and payment meant for Anna, he discovered the awful truth and fell suddenly ill. Calling Anna to him, he berated her, "You sell your novels now, but the time will probably come when you will sell yourself."

Anna's publisher was the famous Russian writer Fyodor Dostoevsky, who had recently returned home from prison and exile in Siberia. Soon Anna's parents reconciled themselves to their daughter's talent, and Dostoevsky called frequently at the Krukovsky home. The forty-two year old writer's moody idealism fascinated the sis-

FYODOR DOSTOEVSKY

ters. At age thirteen, Sophie fell madly in love with him. When he praised her piano playing, she labored to learn Beethoven's *Sonata Pathétique* to please him. But on the day she finally sat down to play the sonata for the man she loved, she looked up after the final note to find the music room deserted. Searching through the house, Sophie spied Dostoevsky seated next to Anna, holding her hand, his face pale. He was proposing marriage. Anna turned him down.

Heartbroken, Sophie returned to her mathematics. At age fourteen, without text or tutor, she taught herself trigonometry—drawing a chord on a circle to understand the sine function and then deriving the other trigonometric functions—to decipher a textbook on optics. The textbook's author, a friend of the family, called her "a second Pascal," and urged Sophie's father to let her study more mathematics. Some time later, the general finally relented and allowed his two daughters to pursue further learning in St. Petersburg.

St. Petersburg was the center of intellectual life in Russia, and Russia was changing. In 1861, when Sophie was eleven, the Tsar had liberated the serfs. New ideas about freedom and fairness were seeping in from the West. But Russian universities did not admit women. Sophie and Anna fervently believed that they could educate themselves for lives of creativity and romance, but only if they could leave Russia.

To leave Russia, a woman needed the permission of her father or husband. Despairing of her father's help, Sophie planned a marriage in name only with a young paleontology student named Vladimir Kovalevsky. One night, as her parents hosted a dinner party, Sophie sneaked out of the house and presented herself at Kovalevsky's lodgings. By the time Sophie's shocked father received the letter she had left him, it was too late. In the general's view, his daughter had compromised herself. He had to consent to the wedding.

Sophie and Vladimir emigrated to Vienna and then to Germany. Sophie's husband, for whom she felt gratitude but not love, refused to move out, and their marriage remained a source of emotional confusion in her life. At nineteen, Sophie audited mathematics courses at the University of Heidelberg. Still, she wanted more, and she applied to the University of Berlin. Once more, she was turned away for being a woman. Desperate, she presented herself in person to the mathematician Karl Weierstrass.

Taken aback at finding a young woman at his door, Weierstrass decided to let her down gently. He gave her a page of difficult problems in elliptical integrals and told her to come back when she had solved them. He thought that would be the end of it. But to his astonishment, the solutions the young lady returned a week later were so clear and original that he felt compelled to offer her a private tutorial. For the next four years, Sophie studied under the personal direction, and eventually the devoted friendship, of one of Europe's leading mathematicians.

TSAR ALEXANDER II

In 1856, Russia lost the Crimean War against Britain, France, and the Ottoman Empire. The war had exposed Russia's backwardness, and her lack of technology and railroads. Two hundred thousand Russian men had died.

*Tsar Alexander II decided it was time for reforms. He abolished serfdom, a kind of feudal slavery that bound peasants to the nobles' land. Land redistribution began. The Tsar allowed local representative government bodies to arise in villages and provinces. These **zemstva** provided education, charity, and other services. Alexander also reformed the armed forces and the justice system.*

Then, in 1881, an assassin with a bomb murdered Alexander in his coach. The liberal Tsar's son, Alexander III, reacted with swift repression. He consolidated power, insisted on the Russification of the empire, and encouraged the persecution of both revolutionaries and Jews. Meanwhile, he continued to build Russian industry, expand the country's transportation system, and grow the economy.

LIBERATION OF THE SERFS BY B. KUSTODIEV

MATHEMATICS

In 1871, Sophie rushed to Paris, where her sister Anna had secretly moved to join the literary life. There Anna had fallen in love with a young French radical who became a leader of the short-lived 1871 Paris Commune. But now the Commune was under military siege, and Anna needed help. Sophie and Vladimir sneaked into the city by stealing a rowboat and rowing across the Seine. Once there, they assisted Anna and the ambulance corps for several weeks before returning to Berlin.

KARL WEIERSTRASS

In 1874, after four years of tutorials, Weierstrass decided that his twenty-four-year-old pupil was ready for a doctorate. Kovalevskaya prepared three treatises, on the rings of Saturn, Abelian integrals, and partial differential equations. Any one of them, Weierstrass felt, merited a degree. Indeed, the University of Göttingen, where she had never attended a single class or passed a single exam, awarded Kovalevskaya a PhD degree *summa cum laude*. Hers was the first doctorate in mathematics ever awarded to a woman in Europe.

PARIS COMMUNE, BARRICADE AT THE PLACE BLANCHE

> *"I was unfortunately weak in the multiplication tables."*

Even Weierstrass, however, could not obtain a professor's position for Sophie. In 1875, she and her husband returned to Russia. There the best job offer Sophie received was teaching arithmetic to elementary school girls. Such a job wouldn't suit her, she wrote, because "I was unfortunately weak in the multiplication tables." For the next several years, Kovalevskaya abandoned all her mathematical work and even stopped answering letters from her old advisor, Weierstrass. Instead she and her husband, living together at last as husband and wife, used Sophie's small inheritance to launch a number of business ventures. Sophie wrote popular science articles, theater reviews, and fiction. She also helped found a girls' school, but because of her supposed radical political views, she was not allowed to teach there.

In 1880, as she turned thirty, Kovalevskaya began working on mathematics again. She presented several papers at a conference, where they were well received. By that time, Kovalevskaya had a two-year-old daughter, but her increasingly moody husband had fallen under the influence of a shady business partner, and the couple separated. Sophie returned to Berlin. Two years later she received the shocking news of her husband's suicide.

Then, in 1883, Gösta Mittag-Leffler, another former student of Weierstrass, invited Sophie Kovalevskaya to give a series of lectures at the University of Stockholm. Not everyone was pleased. The noted playwright August Strindberg wrote to the local paper, "A female professor is a pernicious and unpleasant phenomenon—even, one might say, a monstrosity."

Mittag-Leffler's sister, the novelist Anna Leffler, described Kovalevskaya as striking but not beautiful. She had a large head, prominent hazel eyes, full lips, small hands, and prominent blue veins in her pale skin. Her

Differential equations are equations that relate a variable to how quickly its value is changing. For example, if we know how fast an object accelerates in gravity as it falls to earth, we can calculate its position at any time.

Partial differential equations are used when there are several variables whose effects are to be calculated at once. For example, how are the populations of moose and wolves related? What happens to heat flow through fluids under different pressures? Partial differential equations play an important role in physics, engineering, biology and economics.

Sophie Kovalevskaya's special contribution to partial differential equations was to prove that for a certain class of such equations, a unique solution does exist. Her work became codified in the Cauchy-Kovalevskaya theorem.

GÖSTA MITTAG-LEFFLER

MATHEMATICS

style of dress was negligent, at times almost slovenly. When a mathematical idea took hold of her she dropped everything to work on it. Leffler wrote, "She might be engaged in the most lively conversation at a picnic or party . . . when suddenly a silence would fall upon her. Her look at such times became distant, and her replies, when addressed, wandering. She would suddenly say farewell, and no persuasions, no previous plans or arrangements, no consideration for other people, could detain her. Go home and work she must."

Over time, Sophie's private Stockholm lectures evolved into a permanent, tenured professorship. Kovalevskaya became editor of a mathematics journal and was appointed Chair of Mechanics. She wrote a paper on crystals. Even Russia recognized her at last, electing her the first female member of the Russian Imperial Academy of Sciences.

In 1887, Sophie's beloved sister Anna died in Russia, and Sophie slumped into depression. She revived when a Russian lawyer named Maxim Kovalevsky arrived in Stockholm to give a series of lectures. The two Russian exiles began a passionate love affair. Maxim offered to marry Sophie on the condition that she give up her research. Sophie was torn. Despite her desire for an all-encompassing love, she was wrestling with the most intriguing mathematical challenge of her career. She said no.

The French Academy of Sciences had offered a prize for anyone who could solve a fiendishly difficult problem: mathematically describing the rotational motion of an irregular object. In 1888, Sophie entered her paper "On the Rotation of a Solid Body about a Fixed Point." Her entry addressed the case of a rotating solid object whose center of mass is not on the axis of rotation.

ANNA CARLOTTA LEFFLER

Sophie's theory and solution were so elegant that when she won, the prize committee increased the award from 3000 to 5000 francs. The President of the Academy of Sciences said, "Her work bears witness not only to profound and broad knowledge, but to a mind of great inventiveness."

While completing two more papers on rigid body motion, Sophie also continued her literary pursuits. She collaborated with Anna Leffler to write a long, romantic play called *The Struggle for Happiness*. Maxim Kovalevsky encouraged her to write the autobiographical novels that followed, including *The Sisters Rajevsky* (1889) and *The Nihilist Girl* (1890). Sophie saw no contradiction between being a novelist and being a mathematician. She wrote, "It seems to me that the poet must see what others do not see, must see more deeply than other people. And the mathematician must do the same."

> *"The poet must see what others do not see, must see more deeply than other people. And the mathematician must do the same."*

In 1891, in the full bloom of her career, Kovalevskaya went on holiday to Italy. Upon her return to Sweden, she fell ill with a cough that rapidly worsened into pneumonia. At the age of forty-one, Sophie Kovalevskaya died. The elderly Karl Weierstrass burned her letters and wrote in sorrow, "People die; ideas endure."

Throughout her life, Sophie Kovalevskaya found herself torn between her need for intellectual stimulation and her idealistic notions of what love and life should offer. Intensely romantic, she longed to immerse herself in an all-engulfing love. But repeatedly she rebounded from romantic disappointment to throw herself once more into the "exalted and mysterious science" of mathematics. There she made her lasting mark.

MATHEMATICS

Timeline | 1864-1934

January uprising in Poland is crushed | 1864

1865 | American Civil War ends

Birth of Marie Sklodowska, later Curie | 1867

1876 | Death of Marie's mother

LINCOLN MEMORIAL

STARRY NIGHT BY VAN GOGH

Van Gogh paints Starry Night | 1889

1891 | Enrolls at the Sorbonne

Marries Pierre Curie | 1894

1895 | Roentgen discovers X-rays

Becquerel discovers "uranium rays" | 1896

1898 | Discovery of radium

Receives doctorate and Nobel Prize | 1903

1905 | Einstein's theory of special relativity

Death of Pierre Curie | 1906

1911 | Receives second Nobel Prize

Bohr model of the atom | 1913

1914-18 | World War I

Polish independence from Russia | 1918

1921 | Tour of the United States

$n = 3$

$n = 2$

$n = 1$

$\Delta E = hf$

$+Ze$

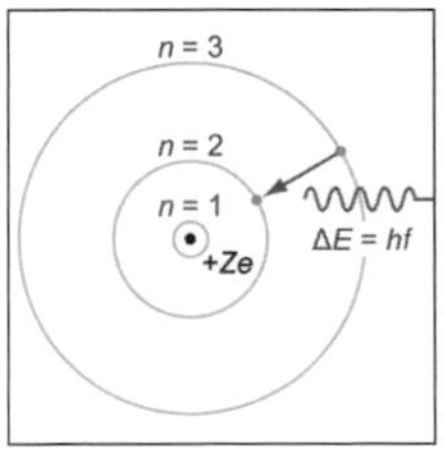

BOHR ATOM

Chadwick discovers the neutron | 1932

NOBEL MEDAL

1934 | Death of Marie Curie

9 | *Radioactivity and the First Woman Nobelist*

Marie Sklodowska Curie

1867-1934 | *Poland and France*

Marie Curie, the most famous Frenchwoman after Joan of Arc, grew up as a Polish patriot. She was born in 1867 in Russian-occupied Poland as the fifth and youngest child in a family of educators and minor nobility. Her father, assistant director of a gymnasium, or high school that prepares students for university, was an enthu-siastic amateur scientist who wrote articles popularizing scientific discoveries, and who loved to explain the ways of nature to his children. On weekends, he taught his children patriotic songs and poetry. But the children considered their mother, who had once headed a girls' private school and now economized by making shoes for her children, the moral head of the family. From her parents, Marie gained both a love of learning and a propensity for hard work.

During Marie's childhood, Russia clamped down on Polish schools, insisting that even private schools teach in Russian and propound the Russian view of history and geography. Secretly, however, the schools taught Polish history and culture, a fact they disguised when the Russian school inspector arrived. Marie was a quick learner with a grave manner, so from the age of six she often found herself selected to recite a Russian lesson for the inspector, a duty she fulfilled with both timidity and patriotic indignation.

MARIE SKLODOWSKA AT SIXTEEN

The Polish-Lithuanian Commonwealth (1569-1795), which lasted over two centuries, was ruled by a parliament of nobles and their elected king. At its peak, the Commonwealth had eleven million citizens and territory which included today's Latvia, Belarus, and most of Ukraine. But in 1795, after a period of military and economic decline, Poland was partitioned among its neighbors Austria, Prussia, and Russia. The **January Uprising** *of 1864, three years before Marie Curie's birth, was crushed after eighteen months and led to fiercer Russian repression. Poland did not regain independence until 1918 at the end of World War I. Twenty-one years later, Hitler's invasion of Poland marked the beginning of World War II and the loss, once more, of Polish independence.*

POLAND'S JANUARY UPRISING

When Marie was four, her mother contracted tuberculosis. In that time before antibiotics, Mrs. Sklodowska's search for a cure meant she spent long periods away from home in distant health resorts. Her letters home alternated between hope and despair at her lack of improvement. Her eldest child Zosia often accompanied her, while her husband and younger children wrote longing letters. Then, in 1874, Zosia died of typhus. After this heartbreak, Marie's mother declined more rapidly, and twenty-seven months later, she too died. Ten-year-old Marie fell into a deep depression that recurred at times throughout her life.

A Russian inspector had fired Marie's father from his school director's job, and although he soon found another teaching post, he also turned the family house into a boarding school to help pay medical bills and make ends meet. Home was a cacophony of students reciting their lessons aloud. Summer vacations with relatives in the country, by contrast, were happy times for Marie, with long nature walks, horseback riding, and dances.

Because women were not allowed to attend university in Poland, Marie and her older sisters dreamed of pursuing higher education abroad. The barrier was lack of money. Their father scraped together enough to send Marie's sister Bronia to Paris, where she studied medicine; Marie, as the younger sister, would have to wait her turn. After graduating first in her class from gymnasium at age fifteen, Marie looked for work. After a miserable year as governess to a lawyer's family in Warsaw, she spent three years teaching the children of the Zorawskis, a landowning family of country nobility. There, with her employer's blessing, she also established a free school for peasant children, a risky and illegal undertaking.

Marie loved the countryside, with its long walks and sleigh rides. The landowner's eldest daughter became a friend, and at night Marie pursued her own studies, focusing on mathematics and physics. But relations with the Zorawskis plummeted when she and their oldest son, a mathematics student at Warsaw University, fell in love. The couple announced their plan to marry, but the Zorawski parents absolutely forbade their son to marry a penniless governess. The son wavered for the next four years, causing Marie a recurring cycle of hope, disappointment, and pain.

"I was taught that the way of progress is neither swift nor easy."

After leaving the Zorawskis, Marie took a third governess position in Warsaw, but a year later she returned to live with her father. To continue her studies, she joined an underground cooperative where young people taught each other in living rooms across Warsaw. The young students were motivated by Polish positivism, the conviction that the best way to serve their oppressed country was by hard work, self-improvement, and sharing knowledge with those who could make the best use of it. To her great delight, Marie also found the chance to try her hand at experiments in a laboratory organized by a cousin. She later wrote of these first attempts, "At times I would be encouraged by a little unhoped-for success, at others I would be in the deepest despair because of accidents and failures resulting from my inexperience. . . . I was taught that the way of progress is neither swift nor easy."

In 1891, at the age of twenty-four, Marie Sklodowska finally traveled to Paris to join her sister Bronia, now a medical doctor, married and expecting her first child. Marie enrolled at the Sorbonne—by that time relatively open to foreign women though still very difficult for Frenchwomen to enter—and rented a garret near the university. She studied mathematics and physics. At first her courses were a struggle, since despite her efforts at self-study, her preparation, particularly in mathematics, was deficient. Long days in the library and nights in her freezing garret brought her success. In 1893 she was certified as competent to practice a profession in science, and a year later she received the same certification in mathematics.

In 1894, Marie also met Pierre Curie. Thirty-five years old, he was already a respected physicist, known for his work in crystals and his discovery of piezo-electricity, the charge created in certain crystals subjected to pressure. In her autobiography, Marie recalled their first meeting, describing Pierre as "a tall young man with auburn hair and large, limpid eyes. I noticed the grave and gentle expression of his face, as well as a certain abandon in his attitude, suggesting the dreamer absorbed

PHYSICS

PIERRE AND MARIE CURIE IN THE LABORATORY

in his reflections." The two fell at once into a long conversation on science and society, and he asked to see her again. Before long, he suggested marriage and a life together devoted to science. Because she still longed to return to Poland, Marie hesitated, but after a long vacation at home she returned to Paris, and the couple married in July, 1895. They used a gift of money from a relative to buy two bicycles and took the first of many holidays bicycling through the French countryside.

The new couple were devoted to one another. Marie Curie looked up to Pierre not only for his scientific clarity but for his selfless generosity, his forward-thinking social views, and his unconcern with worldly success. Pierre considered his new wife his equal in everything. He called her his companion and "the soul of my work." In 1897 they welcomed their daughter Irène, who grew up to be a Nobel Prize-winning physicist herself. Around the time of Irène's birth, Pierre's father, Dr. Eugène Curie, came to live with them. He helped to raise their daughter while the couple spent long hours in the laboratory.

In their laboratory in a corner of the school where Pierre taught, he pursued his work on crystals while Marie completed a survey of the magnetic properties of differently tempered steels, which she published in 1897. With that done, she began to think about a topic for a doctoral thesis. In consultation with her husband, she settled on a strange new phenomenon, uranium rays.

In 1895, William Roentgen had discovered X-rays. These are the form of electromagnetic radiation created when a high energy beam of electrons strikes a substance, particularly a metal. The rays can escape from a vacuum tube, penetrate matter, and leave a shadowed image on a photographic plate. A French scientist, Henri Becquerel, next discovered that certain uranium salts, when placed on black paper overlying a photographic plate, also gave off rays that penetrated the paper and exposed the plate. At first he thought that the uranium was merely re-emitting light it had absorbed earlier, but after an experiment where he kept the uranium in a dark cupboard for several days before trying its powers, he determined that this was not the case: the uranium gave off rays all on its own. Intrigued, the 73-year-old Lord Kelvin in England showed that uranium rays, like X-rays, electrified air in a measurable way. But after a brief flurry of interest, the scientific community gave no further attention to uranium. X-rays seemed much more exciting.

Marie Curie decided to investigate uranium rays further. She and Pierre set up a device that allowed them to measure the efficiency with which a mineral electrified the air. Then Marie began a series of careful measurements, first on uranium salts and then on other elements and minerals she scavenged from friends. Gold, copper, and eleven other elements gave off no rays. But to her surprise, she found that a heavy, black uranium ore called pitchblende showed activity even greater than pure uranium's. Marie deduced correctly that this result meant pitchblende contained another, unknown, element whose activity—she gave it the name radio-activity—was much greater than that of uranium. A short time later, she discovered that the element thorium, too, was more radioactive than uranium, although pitchblende contained some substance more radioactive still.

In her first report to the French Academy of Sciences about her discoveries, Marie Curie made two important points. First, radioactivity was an atomic property of certain elements. Radioactivity increased proportionally with the amount of uranium or thorium tested, and conditions of temperature or chemical combination did not affect it. Secondly, radioactivity itself could indicate the presence of an unknown element.

By this time, Pierre Curie had abandoned his study of crystals to join his wife in her subject of research. The two of them understood that to convince the scientific world of their discovery, they needed to isolate the new element contained in pitchblende. To do so they pulverized large quantities of pitchblende and worked to separate its elements chemically. At each stage of separation, they tested the two separated products to see which was more radioactive. The more radioactive product was the fraction that contained their new, highly radioactive, element.

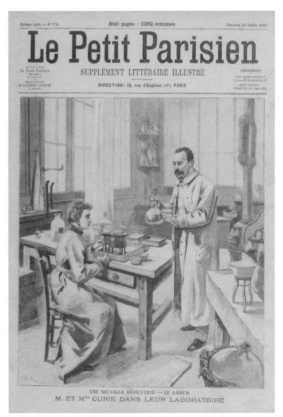

To test the purity of their preparation, they used spectroscopy, heating the preparation and examining through a prism the light it emitted. The number of spectral lines continued to tell them their substance was not pure, even as its radioactivity increased to more than three hundred times the activity of uranium.

By this time, the Curies had discovered not one, but two separate highly radioactive fractions from their analysis of pitchblende. The first, which co-precipitated with bismuth, they named polonium in honor of Marie's native country. The second, which accompanied barium, they eventually named radium. With radium, purified to the point that it had 900 times the activity of uranium,

DRAWING FROM A POPULAR PARIS NEWSPAPER, COURTESY OF RONALD SMELTZER

they eventually found a bright red spectral line that belonged to no known element. In 1898, in recognition of her work, the Academy awarded Marie Curie a prize of 3800 francs, though instead of informing her directly, the academicians wrote letters to her husband informing *him*.

"Faint, fairy lights."

Once they had established the existence of radium, Pierre and Marie Curie pursued different paths in their research. Marie undertook to purify the new element in order to determine its atomic weight and its place in the periodic table, while Pierre investigated the physical nature of the "rays" they had discovered. Marie wrote later that she might never have taken on the task of purifying radium if she had known how difficult it would be. She begged for residues from uranium processing plants and received loads of discarded brown dust mixed with pine needles. The work took place in an old hangar with a leaky roof. Marie Curie later wrote:

> . . . It was in this miserable old shed that we passed the best and happiest years of our life, devoting our entire days to our work. . . . Sometimes I had to spend a whole day mixing a boiling mass with a heavy iron rod nearly as large as myself. . . . Other days, on the contrary, the work would be a most minute and delicate fractional distillation. . . . I was then annoyed by the floating dust of iron and coal from which I could not protect my precious products. But I shall never be able to express the joy of the untroubled quietness of this atmosphere of research and the excitement of actual progress. . . . One of our joys was to go into our workroom at night; we then perceived on all sides the feebly luminous silhouettes of the bottles or capsules containing our products. . . . The glowing tubes looked like faint, fairy lights.

Finally, in 1902, Marie Curie succeeded in extracting, from one ton of pitchblende, one-tenth of a gram of radium. She estimated its atomic weight to be 226. The following year she received her doctorate for a PhD thesis based on her work with radium. That year, too, the Curies were informed that, along with Henri Becquerel, they were to be awarded the Nobel Prize in Physics for their radioactivity work. The prize brought money as well as recognition, but both Curies were exhausted and often ill—no doubt as a result of their heavy radiation exposure—and they did not manage to travel to Stockholm to receive their honors until 1905.

With the awarding of the Nobel Prize, the Curies became the darlings of the French press. Unexpected visitors barged in on them at work and at home, and when journalists couldn't get an interview, they happily made one up. Articles were written about the romance of the Curies' life in science and their magnanimous decision not to patent their processes for extracting radium. Radium itself caught the public imagination, which endowed the faintly glowing blue material with miraculous properties as a possible cure for everything from rheumatism to cancer. All the attention disrupted the Curies' routine and particularly annoyed Pierre, who complained that he could no longer work with so many interruptions.

In 1904, Pierre Curie was appointed as professor to a new physics chair at the Sorbonne, and Marie was appointed chief of his laboratory—although the laboratory did not yet exist. At the same time, she began teaching physics to young women at a teachers' college in Sèvres, where she revamped the curriculum and added laboratory experience. That year, too, the Curies welcomed their second child, Eve, who grew up to be a talented musician and her mother's biographer.

Prospects were good for the Curies in 1906. Despite their shared fatigue and Pierre's poor health, they looked forward to having an adequate laboratory at last. Meanwhile, in their corner laboratory, Pierre Curie measured the heat radium emitted, while he and Marie speculated on the source of that heat. Did radium somehow absorb energy from outside, or did energy come from a breakdown of radium atoms themselves? Pierre mulled these questions over as he took Irène on long walks on the beach or in the countryside. He roused himself from his reverie to point out plants and animals, teaching her natural history. And then, walking home from his publisher's one stormy day, probably lost in thought, Pierre fell under the wheels of a horse-drawn wagon and was instantly killed.

Marie Curie was devastated. Although she kept a calm facade as letters and tributes flowed in from around the world, she poured her own grief into a journal addressed to her lost husband. She wrote, "In the street I walk as though hypnotized, without care about anything. I will not kill myself, I don't even have the desire for suicide. But among all these carriages, isn't there one that will make me share the fate of my beloved?" The loss of her best friend and collaborator made her doubt she could even continue in science. But within a month, with her sister visiting to care for the children, Marie Curie once more sought the tranquility of the laboratory. She divided her time among the children, the laboratory, and visits to the cemetery.

In the wake of Pierre's death, the faculty of the Sorbonne took an unprecedented step by asking Marie Curie to take over her husband's physics course. She would be the first woman professor in the university's centuries-long history. Curie agreed on the condition that her female students from Sèvres could attend. Crowds filled the room and spilled out of doors on the afternoon of her first lecture. One student remembered Curie that day as very pale, "her face impassive, her black dress extremely simple; one saw only her luminous, large forehead, crowned by abundant and filmy ashen blonde hair, which she pulled back tight without succeeding in hiding her beauty." Without

FIRST LECTURE BY A WOMAN AT THE SORBONNE. NOTE THE FADED IMAGE OF PIERRE CURIE IN THE BACKGROUND. COURTESY OF RONALD SMELTZER.

drawing attention to herself by remarking on the occasion or memorializing her husband, Curie simply began, "When one considers the progress in physics in the last decade, one is surprised by the changes it has produced in our ideas about electricity and about matter." Many in the audience found themselves in tears.

For two years, Marie Curie wore black and kept to herself. She and Pierre's father, who continued to help care for the little girls, moved to a cottage in the suburb of Sceaux, where he kept a garden and she could easily visit the cemetery. Marie helped to organize a school for the children of the Sorbonne professors who lived nearby. She collected her Sorbonne lectures into a thousand-page *Treatise on Radioactivity*. Then, perhaps through the children's cooperative school, Curie developed a close friendship with Paul Langevin, a talented physicist and former student of Pierre's. The father of four and unhappily married, Langevin came to Marie at first for sympathy and advice, but eventually their friendship developed into a love affair. Once again Marie Curie glimpsed the possibility of a partnership of love and physics. The dream unraveled when Langevin allowed his abusive wife, not once but twice, to discover letters from his lover. Mrs. Langevin threatened to kill Marie, who truly feared for her life.

MARIE, EVE, AND IRÈNE CURIE

In 1911, friends persuaded Curie to submit her name for membership in the French Academy of Sciences, where she might become the first woman member. Partly as a result of opposition from the right-wing press, her candidacy was defeated. She never tried for membership again, though many foreign academies of science made her a member. That same year, by invitation, Curie attended the first of the prestigious Solvay conferences in physics. While she was in Belgium for the conference, the gutter press broke the story of her affair with Langevin, vilifying Curie as a foreign woman breaking up the home of a virtuous French mother.

Marie Curie's friends and colleagues rushed to her defense, in person and in the press. Two days after the first press reports of the affair, the Swedish Academy voted to award Marie Curie a second Nobel Prize, this one in chemistry, for her discovery of radium and polonium. This time, indignant French newspapers made no mention of the prize. Then, in November, after a series of scurrilous articles, one French newspaper published excerpts of Curie's letters to Langevin. Immediately, Langevin challenged the editor to a duel, which luckily passed off with no shots fired.

At that point, Svante Arrhenius of the Swedish Academy wrote to Curie suggesting that it would be inappropriate for her to collect the Nobel Prize in person, saying that if they had known of the letters, the Academy would probably never have awarded her the prize. With her personal morality under attack, Curie responded acidly, "The action which you advise would appear to be a grave error on my part. In fact the prize has been awarded for the discovery of Radium and Polonium. I believe that there is no connection between my scientific work and the facts of private life." She traveled to Stockholm, where she received the prize from King Gustaf without awkwardness. Then she went home and collapsed.

For the next couple of years, Marie Curie suffered from recurrent pyelonephritis, infection of the kidney, leading to fever, pain, and pus in the urine. Without antibiotics, she had no choice but to travel to various resorts seeking a rest cure, as her mother had done for tuberculosis. But unlike her mother, Curie gradually recovered sufficiently to write papers, supervise work in her laboratory, follow the construction of the new Radium Institute, and work with Ernest Rutherford on creating an international radium standard by which to measure the activity and purity of other radium samples.

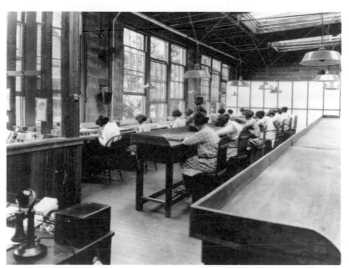

RADIUM GIRLS AT WORK

Radium seemed like such a miraculous element that doctors and businessmen rushed to exploit its possible applications. Radium creams or baths were used to treat skin conditions such as eczema or the rash of lupus, while radium salts were used to treat a variety of cancers, and patients inhaled radon gas, a breakdown product, for lung infections such as tuberculosis. Meanwhile, businessmen created radium toothpaste—guaranteed to whiten teeth—radium bath salts, radium-infused drinks, radium hair creams, and glowing radium watch dials.

Most of these treatments were worse than useless. Radium emits radiation which damages cells and disrupts DNA. Such disruption can lead to cancer or to severe anemia due to death of cells in the bone marrow. In 1928, the case of five "Radium Girls" caught public attention. These women, hired to paint radium on watch dials, had been instructed to lick their paintbrushes to keep them sharp, even as their employers were careful to wear lead aprons and maintain their distance from the radium. The women, who later suffered cancer, fractures, and necrosis of the jaw, successfully sued their employers, helping to establish the first occupational safety laws in America.

PHYSICS

When World War I arrived in August 1914, Marie Curie thought at once about how to help her adopted nation. Military hospitals were springing up throughout France to accommodate the huge number of war wounded, and few of them had adequate X-ray equipment. Curie set herself to organize a radiologic service, collecting and installing X-ray machines and training volunteers in their use. With the help of the Red Cross, she equipped a mobile X-ray lab in a donated van that could be driven close to the battlefields where it was needed. Assisted by Irène, now seventeen, Curie performed thousands of X-rays to document broken bones and locate pieces of shrapnel before surgery. By the end of the war, the Curies had completed two hundred hospital installations and equipped twenty X-ray cars. They had traveled all over the country under difficult conditions and worked endless hours alongside medical personnel and other volunteers. Because the men they trained in radiology were so often called to other duties, the Curies also added a radiology course for nurses at the Radium Institute in Paris. Irène taught the nurses even as she completed her own degree in physics at the Sorbonne.

> *"To hate the very idea of war . . ."*

Reminiscing after the war, Marie Curie wrote, "To hate the very idea of war, it ought to be sufficient to see what I have seen so many times, all through these years: men and boys brought to the advanced ambulance in a mixture of mud and blood, many of them dying of their injuries, many others recovering but slowly through months of pain and suffering." Yet the war brought Marie Curie one great joy: the Treaty of Versailles made Poland free and independent at last.

Curie spent the years after the war building and strengthening the Radium Institute, raising money and overseeing students and visiting scientists. The Institute included one laboratory devoted to physical and chemical research and a second laboratory, headed by Dr. Claudius Regaud, dedicated to exploring radium's therapeutic potential for treating cancers and other diseases. In 1920, Curie met the American journalist, Mary Meloney. Captivated by the story of the modest French widow toiling in poverty—a gross exaggeration—Meloney organized a campaign to raise $100,000 from the women of America to buy Marie Curie a gram of radium. The campaign was successful, and in 1921 Marie and Irène arrived for an exhausting gala tour of the United States, peppered with press appearances and honorary degrees and culminating with the gift of radium from President Harding. For Marie Curie, highlights of the trip included Niagara Falls, the Grand Canyon, and visits to women's colleges. Modest and retiring in her simple black dress, Curie proved to be an excellent international symbol of science and a prodigious fundraiser.

RADIOLOGY AND WAR,
COURTESY OF
RONALD SMELTZER

In the 1920s, Curie used the organizational skills she had honed during the war to fill the Radium Institute with researchers and equipment. She reserved a certain number of places in the laboratory each year for women and foreigners. Curie's own research focused on clarifying the process of radioactive decay, but the Institute's most important advances were made by others: Marguerite Perey discovered francium and Irène and her husband Frédéric Joliot discovered artificial radioactivity.

During the 1920s, evidence accumulated about the health hazards of radioactivity. Researchers in the Radium Institute and other laboratories around the world fell ill or even died with unsettling frequency. Curie made her researchers undergo frequent blood tests and take time off in the country when the test results were abnormal: she had a stubborn faith in the curative powers of fresh air, pointing to her own long life as evidence that radium was not so harmful after all. She continued to swim, ice skate, and walk in the country. However, in 1934, at the age of 67, as she sought yet another rest cure in the French Alps, Marie Curie succumbed to "extreme pernicious anemia"— likely either leukemia or aplastic anemia, and almost certainly caused by prolonged exposure to radiation. Her funeral was a simple one, and she was laid to rest with her beloved Pierre in the cemetery at Sceaux. Later, the remains of both scientists were removed to lie among other French heroes in the Pantheon.

Marie Curie, passionate, stubborn, and devoted to the idea that science could improve the world, was the first woman scientist of the twentieth century to achieve international renown. Her discovery of radioactive elements launched a branch of physics and chemistry that ultimately gave birth to a new field, nuclear physics. Key to this new direction was Curie's insight that radioactivity was an atomic property, not a chemical one. This understanding led to a re-conception of the atom as a particle made up of other, more fundamental particles that could break apart, leading to atomic and elemental change.

PHYSICS

Timeline | 1878-1992

Birth of Lise Meitner | 1878

THE SCREAM BY
EDVARD MUNCH

EINSTEIN

1893 | Edvard Mumch
paints The Scream

Curies discover | 1898
radium

1901 | Admitted to university

Begins research on | 1907
radioactivity with
Otto Hahn

1913 | Bohr atom proposed

Einstein's general theory of relativity | 1916
Meitner isolates protactinium | 1918

1914-18 | World War I

1932 | Chadwick discovers the neutron

Jewish professors fired from | 1933
German universities

Meitner flees to Sweden | 1938

1938 | Anschluss: Germany annexes Austria

Discovery of nuclear fission | 1939

Fission bombs dropped on Hiroshima | 1945
and Nagasaki

1939-45 | World War II

ATOMIC BOMB

1956 | First neutrinos
detected

1966 | Receives Enrico
Fermi award

Death of Lise | 1968
Meitner

HITLER

1992 | Discovery of meitnerium

10 | *The Physics of Fission*

Lise Meitner

1878-1968 | *Austria*

LISE MEITNER AS A YOUNG WOMAN

The Nobel Prize ceremonies of November 1946 presented a painful challenge to Lise Meitner, co-discoverer of nuclear fission. In exile from Germany since 1938, she lived in Stockholm, so she was determined to welcome her dear friend Otto Hahn as he came to collect his solo Nobel Prize in Chemistry. Yet it stung that he alone was receiving the prize for work the two of them had conceived and pursued together for so many years.

In some ways worse than the Nobel Prize committee's neglect was Hahn's attitude. He failed to acknowledge Meitner's contribution just as he failed to shoulder any responsibility for the great harm Germany had done during World War II. Meitner wrote later that Otto was "simply suppressing the past . . . I am part of that suppressed past." Nevertheless, Meitner showed her steadfastness. She attended the prize ceremony and arranged dinner parties for Hahn and his wife. She did not complain aloud even when the press dismissively referred to her as Hahn's one-time assistant.

Lise Meitner grew up in Vienna, Austria, the third of eight children. Her parents were secular Jews, her mother a musician and her father a lawyer. Lise's older sister, Gusti, was musically gifted; she became a concert pianist and composer. Though Lise loved music all her life, her gifts turned another way. She slept with a mathematics book under her pillow. And she wondered. Once her religious grandmother told her that sewing on the Sabbath was so wicked it would make the sky fall. Timidly, the young Lise poked a needle into her embroidery. Nothing. She made one furtive stitch. The sky stayed up. Soon Lise was sewing furiously, having tested and proved false her grandmother's dire warning.

Another time, struck by the beautiful colors a few drops of oil made on the surface of a puddle, Lise asked how it happened. Her father's answer, about how interference patterns of light reflecting off a thin film lead to the display of color we call iridescence, fired her with a desire to understand more. But in Austria in the nineteenth century, public education for girls ended at fourteen. The only profession open to females was teaching. Reluctantly, Lise took a private course preparing her to teach French in a girls' school. She tutored young girls to help pay for Gusti's music lessons, and she volunteered with relief organizations.

Then, when Lise Meitner was nineteen, Austrian universities opened to women who could pass the entrance exam, a difficult challenge for girls who had not attended high school. Following her father's advice, Meitner completed her teacher training. Then, with several other girls who joined together to study, she crammed four or more years of university preparation into just two years. Fourteen women took the entrance exam in 1901, but Meitner was one of only four to pass.

MAX PLANCK, FATHER OF QUANTUM THEORY

She studied with the ardent physicist Ludwig Boltzmann, who asked of his students "strict attention, iron discipline, tireless strength of mind." Meitner's nephew Otto Frisch later wrote, "Boltzmann gave her the vision of physics as a battle for ultimate truth, a vision she never lost."

Only the second woman in Germany to earn a physics doctorate, Lise Meitner could not find a job in physics. She taught French during the day and volunteered in a lab studying radiation at night, eventually publishing two papers. Finally Max Planck in Berlin agreed to accept her as a research student. Planck's own belief at the time was that the rare talented woman should be offered a chance to learn, but that "nature itself has designated for woman her vocation as mother and housewife." Too much education, Planck believed, would lead to congenital weakness in the woman's offspring.

In Berlin's profoundly male environment, Lise Meitner, age twenty-eight, found herself almost paralyzed by shyness. Still, she forced herself to extend the theoretical physics she learned in Planck's lectures by seeking work in a physics laboratory. In 1907 she began collaborating on studies in radioactivity with chemist Otto Hahn. Otto was her own age, charming, informal, and outgoing. The two of them worked together extremely well. Hahn was an exacting, detail-oriented chemist; Meitner was a physicist with a gift for choosing problems where theory and experiment could push one another forward.

For the first two years of her work with Hahn, Meitner never entered his laboratory. Emil Fischer, director of the laboratory, did not allow women in his chemistry building, ostensibly because he worried that their hair would be a fire hazard. Meitner did her experiments in the basement and walked down the street to a hotel when she needed a bathroom. Then, in

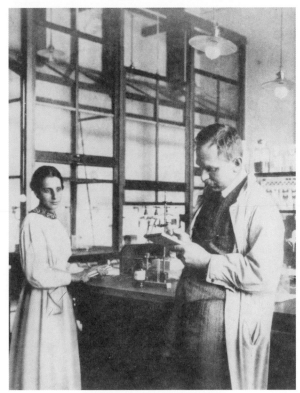

LISE MEITNER AND OTTO HAHN IN THE LABORATORY

1909, Fischer relented. Though she still worked in the basement, Meitner was allowed to attend conferences and discussions upstairs.

For six years Meitner served as an unpaid guest researcher, living on a small allowance from

EMIL FISCHER, ORGANIC CHEMIST

her father and often surviving on toast and tea. By 1912, she had more than twenty publications to her name, with Hahn almost always listed as first author. That year, Max Planck made her a paid assistant. She helped grade student papers, and she began to feel like a respected member of the circle of physicists around Planck. Evenings at Planck's house included music and games of tag, with Einstein playing violin and Lise teaching Brahms songs to the other scientists.

In 1913 Fischer, who had once confined Meitner to the basement, made her an associate of the new Kaiser Wilhelm Institute for Chemistry. Her rank was now equal to Hahn's, and together they ran the radioactivity division of the institute. There they continued their five-year search for the precursor element to actinium, a radioactive element that formed part of the decay series, or breakdown elements, of uranium.

When World War I broke out, most of the young men of the institute joined the army. Hahn was among them. Before long he was assigned to Fritz Haber's secret chemical warfare unit. Meitner, on the other hand, moved by patriotism and inspired by Marie Curie's work on the "enemy" side, underwent training as a nurse and X-ray technician, and served near the Russian front. She performed more than a thousand X-rays, repaired electrical equipment, and assisted in the operating room. The suffering she witnessed turned her against war. She wrote to a friend, "These poor people, who will at best be cripples, have the most horrible pains. One can hear their screams and groans as well as see their horrible wounds. . . . One has one's own thoughts about war when one sees all this."

In 1916, no longer needed at the front, Meitner resumed her work with actinium. She kept Hahn closely involved through a series of letters, and he visited the laboratory whenever he had leave. By the end of the war, Meitner succeeded in isolating protactinium, element number 91, filling a gap between uranium and thorium in the periodic table. As was their custom for chemistry papers, she put Hahn's name first on the paper announcing the discovery. In 1919, the Association of German Chemists awarded Otto Hahn its Emil Fischer Award for the discovery. For Meitner they made a copy of Hahn's medal to keep for herself.

By the end of the war, at age 41, Meitner had been named head of a new physics department at the Kaiser Wilhelm Institute. In 1922, named a Privatdozent (lecturer) and professor, Meitner gave her first public university lecture, titled "The Significance of Radioactivity for Cosmic Processes." A clumsy newspaperman reported it as "Cosmetic Processes." No longer shy, Meitner ran her laboratory with strict rules to prevent radioactive contamination that would make experiments impossible.

LISE MEITNER LECTURING

In the years after the war, Hahn and Meitner branched into different lines of research. He continued to identify radiochemicals, while Meitner pursued numerous problems of nuclear physics. She concentrated primarily on the spectra emitted by beta (electron) radiation from the nucleus. In the 1920s and early 1930s, her reputation eclipsed Hahn's, though the two of them together were nominated almost every year for the Nobel Prize.

When Adolf Hitler came to power in 1933, anti-Semitism became official state policy in Germany. Hitler ordered all Jewish professors fired from the universities. Although Meitner had been baptized a Protestant in 1908, she lost her university appointment. Otto Hahn resigned his own appointment in protest. Still, Meitner was not too worried. The Kaiser Wilhelm Institute where she and Hahn worked was privately funded, and because she was an Austrian citizen she could keep her appointment there. She could still do physics: that was all that mattered.

In Rome, Enrico Fermi had found something intriguing. Bombarding uranium with streams of neutrons, he found new particles that he hypothesized made up a new "transuranic" element, perhaps element number 93. (Uranium was 92.) Immediately interested, Meitner invited Hahn to join her in pursuing this new line of investigation. She needed a radiochemist to help her identify any new and heavy elements. Another young chemist, Fritz Strassmann, joined them. For the next five years, they competed with Fermi's lab in Italy and Irène Joliot-Curie's lab in Paris to create and characterize new elements. All three labs believed that any nuclear changes would be small, changing an element's position on the Periodic Table by only one or two steps. Thus, for years, all three struggled to characterize new, heavy atoms without considering the possibility that the uranium nucleus was actually splitting in two.

Meanwhile, the atmosphere for scholars, and especially Jewish scholars, grew steadily worse in Germany. Hitler and his nationalist followers demanded "Aryan science" unpolluted by such Jewish ideas as relativity. Einstein, on a lecture tour in America, decided not to return. The Jewish editor of a major scientific journal was dismissed and later committed suicide. Meitner was no longer allowed to attend her beloved Wednesday physics symposia, and when presenting their work outside the Institute, Hahn no longer dared mention her name. Hahn even briefly asked Meitner to leave the Institute, but he changed his mind when Max Planck encouraged her to stay.

Then, in April 1938, the German army marched into Austria and annexed the country. Overnight, Meitner lost her protection as an Austrian citizen. Fellow physicists began to seek a position for her outside the country. Friends abroad invited her to come give seminars and talks. But her Austrian passport was no longer valid, which made entering another country a problem. Then Germany announced that Jewish scientists would no longer be allowed to travel abroad. Two physicists, Niels Bohr in Denmark and Dirk Coster in Holland, scram-

On March 11, 1938, members of the Austrian Nazi Party staged a coup d'état in advance of a planned referendum on union with Germany. The Austrian Party took over state institutions and handed power over to Germany. German troops marched into Austria and took over. One month later, the Nazis held a vote to see whether the Austrian people approved the move; they claimed that more than 99% of Austrians voted "yes." This annexation of Austria by Germany is known as the **Anschluss**.

bled to find support for Meitner. Coster traveled to Berlin to rescue her. Packing lightly, Lise left with him on a train for the Dutch border. At the last minute, Hahn gave her his mother's diamond ring to use in case of emergency or to bribe the border guards if necessary. Meitner illegally crossed the border just in time: a spying neighbor had just denounced her to the authorities as someone planning to flee.

Niels Bohr arranged a position for Lise at the Research Institute of Physics in Stockholm, where she had previously taught a course on radioactivity. Manne Siegbahn, a Nobel Prize winner who was building Europe's first cyclotron, would be her host. Unfortunately, Siegbahn took a dislike to Meitner. He gave her laboratory space but no equipment, no assistant, and almost no salary. When students arrived to work with her, he diverted them to work with him instead. At age 59, bereft of friends, family, and possessions, Meitner found herself also stripped of the opportunity to do physics. She wrote to Hahn that she felt like a mechanical doll.

> *We have experienced many surprises in nuclear physics . . ."*

In a reverse of their positions during the First World War, Hahn pushed their research forward, while consulting Meitner about his continuing experiments. One of the bombardment products, he wrote in December 1938, looked like barium, element 56. He could not understand it and needed her advice. "Perhaps you can propose some fantastic explanation. We know ourselves that it can't decay into barium." Two days later, Meitner wrote back, "Your radium results are very puzzling. . . . However, we have experienced many surprises in nuclear physics, so that one cannot say without further consideration that it is impossible." Reassured, Hahn hastened to publish his finding.

OTTO ROBERT FRISCH AT THE PIANO

Over the New Year holiday, Meitner met with her nephew Otto Robert Frisch at a resort town in western Sweden. Frisch was a fine pianist, who liked to cheer up his aunt by playing duets with her. When Meitner couldn't keep up with him on a piece whose tempo was marked "*Allegro ma non tanto*," Otto Robert teased her that the translation was, "Quickly, but not for Auntie."

Frisch was also a nuclear physicist, currently working with Bohr in Copenhagen. On one long outing, while Frisch skied and his aunt kept up by walking alongside, she told him about the puzzling finding. Barium was much too small to create by knocking a few protons and neutrons off uranium's nucleus. And the neutron stream was surely not strong enough to crack a nucleus in two. Unless . . . Niels Bohr had suggested a model of the nucleus like a drop of liquid. Could it stretch, deform like a water balloon into a two-lobed shape, and snap in the middle? If it did, a burst of energy would be released according to Einstein's formula, $E=mc^2$.

In the woods, on scraps of paper, they scribbled down the math. Enough energy would be released to drive the two new atoms apart. They knew what experiment needed to be done. Frisch would do it.

Back in Copenhagen, when Frisch told Niels Bohr about their idea, Bohr struck his forehead, crying, "Oh, what idiots we have all been!" Promising to tell nobody, he immediately left for America. But on the transatlantic crossing, he worked on the mathematics of the new discovery with a fellow physicist who, once they reached America, spread the word. At once several laboratories jumped into the race to prove that the nucleus split. Meanwhile, Otto Frisch carefully repeated his experiment and measurements. He asked a biologist what it was called when a cell split in two. "Fission," the biologist told him, and Frisch named the process of splitting an atom "nuclear fission."

In **nuclear fission**, neutron bombardment of a heavy radioactive element makes it break into two lighter elements, releasing radiation, energy, and a number of fast-moving neutrons. These neutrons can then strike other heavy atoms, breaking them apart in turn. If the resulting chain reaction is controlled and slow, it can produce nuclear energy for use as a power source. If, however, the chain reaction is allowed to proceed without controls, the number of splitting atoms increases exponentially. The explosive energy release that results creates an extremely powerful bomb, such as those the U.S. dropped on Hiroshima and Nagasaki.

PHYSICS

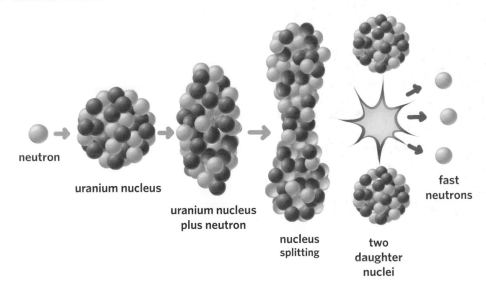

neutron

uranium nucleus

uranium nucleus
plus neutron

nucleus
splitting

two
daughter
nuclei

fast
neutrons

NUCLEAR FISSION

> *"One has one's own thoughts about war"*

Physicists on both sides of the Atlantic quickly realized that nuclear fission, the first process to release more energy than was used to create it, meant that, in theory, "a device of vast and destructive power" could be built. The Americans asked Lise Meitner to join the Manhattan Project but, remembering the suffering of the Great War, she declined. Instead she remained in Sweden, isolated, unable to do follow-up experiments. She watched and worried as Denmark, France, and Holland fell to the German army, putting so many of her friends in danger. She sent food to her rescuer Dirk Coster's family in Holland and to her own family in Austria.

In 1945, as the war in Europe approached its end, Meitner was sickened to learn of the concentration camps. A few months later, news of the atomic bombs falling on Hiroshima and Nagasaki horrified her. When the American popular press briefly celebrated her for her role in research leading to the bomb, Meitner wanted none of it. She said, "I myself have not in any way worked on the smashing of the atom with the idea of producing death-dealing weapons. You must not blame us scientists for the use to which war technicians have put our discoveries." That year the Nobel Committee considered her for a Nobel Prize in physics, but her Swedish nemesis, Manne Siegbahn, probably blocked the nomination. The following year, Meitner hosted Otto Hahn as he accepted his Nobel Prize in chemistry. Hahn insisted that physics had played no role in his discovery.

LISE MEITNER

After the war, Meitner remained in Sweden. Her working conditions improved. In 1947, she declined an invitation from Strassmann to come back and direct her old institute. The chasm between those who had left Germany and those who had stayed, she feared, would be too great. She toured America several times, lecturing and visiting relatives. She taught, climbed mountains, enjoyed music, and, despite her disappointments, remained friendly with Hahn. In 1960, she retired and moved to Cambridge, England, to be near her nephew, Otto Robert Frisch. Although she never complained publicly about the Nobel Prize, or about how her name was being erased from the history of physics, she left behind papers and letters that told her side of the story.

In 1966 the U.S. Atomic Energy Commission awarded its Enrico Fermi Award to non-Americans for the first time: to the whole team of Meitner, Strassmann and Hahn. Two years later, just shy of her ninetieth birthday, Lise Meitner died. In 1992, German scientists fused bismuth and iron into the heaviest known metal, element 109. In honor of Lise Meitner's "fundamental work on the physical understanding of fission," they named the new element meitnerium.

PHYSICS

Timeline | 1882-1939

SOPHIE
KOVALEVSKAYA

1882 | *Birth of Emmy Noether*

Sofia Kovalevskaya wins mathematics | 1888
prize from French Academy

Curies discover radium | 1898

Enrolls at Erlangen | 1904

1903 | *Bohr atom*
proposed

1907 | *Receives*
mathematics PhD

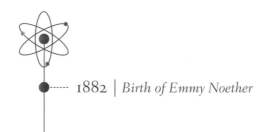

BLUE HORSES BY
FRANZ MARC

Teaches without | 1908-15
pay at Erlangen

Einstein's general | 1916
theory of relativity

1911 | *Franz Marc*
paints Blue Horses

1915 | *Invited to Göttingen; helps Einstein*

1914-18 | *World War I*

Lectures under her own name | 1919
Associate professor without tenure | 1922

WWI POSTER

Gödel's incompleteness theorem | 1931
Noether moves to Bryn Mawr | 1933
Death of Emmy Noether | 1935

World War II begins | 1939

1930 | *van der Waerden's* Moderne Algebra

1932 | *Wins Ackerman-Teubner Memorial*
mathematics prize

1933 | *Hitler chancellor of Germany;*
Jewish professors dismissed

Emmy Noether

1882-1935 | *Germany*

EMMY NOETHER

Enthusiastic and loud, short and overweight, Emmy Noether met no one's standards of an elegant lady. She loved mathematics with all her heart, and when she was discussing it, manners fell out the window. Algebraist Olga Taussky described Noether's behavior at a luncheon where, discussing mathematics, she "gesticulated wildly." When food spilled all over her dress, Emmy just wiped it off and kept talking. Once, during a break in a lecture, two female students tried to get her to neaten her dress and hair. Noether waved them off. She didn't have time. She was talking mathematics to a circle of students.

During Emmy's German childhood, no one expected anything unusual from her. She was the first of four children in a well-off Jewish family. Her father's family dealt in iron imports and her mother's in wholesale goods. Left with a limp by childhood polio, her father, Max Noether, became a mathematics professor in Erlangen, Germany. As a child Emmy was sturdy, nearsighted, clever and friendly. She spoke with a slight lisp. One anecdote tells of her being the only child at a birthday party to solve a brainteaser requiring logic. Other than that, she showed her family no sign of being exceptionally gifted. She took piano lessons and loved to dance.

In Germany at the end of the nineteenth century, higher education and even academic high schools were not open to women. Emmy followed family expectations by attending a teacher preparation program. At eighteen she scored "very good" on a five-day examination that qualified her to teach French and English to girls. But then she did something unexpected. Instead of seeking a teaching position, she spent two years auditing courses at her father's university. Only two years earlier, the faculty senate had rejected mixed-sex education because it would "overthrow all academic order," so she had to get the individual permission of professors to sit in on their classes. Luckily, most of them were family friends.

In July 1903, as a result of her studies, Emmy was able to pass the university entrance exam. Still, at most universities she could only audit courses, not receive credit or gain a degree. At the age of twenty-one, Emmy decided to move to Göttingen and study mathematics with Felix Klein, a great advocate for women. He was the inventor of the Klein bottle, which is a three-dimensional analogue of the Mobius strip. In 1904, when Erlangen, her father's university, finally decided to enroll women, Noether transferred back. She became one of only eighty women in all of Germany studying for a university degree in any subject.

KLEIN BOTTLE, A THREE DIMENSIONAL OBJECT WITH A SINGLE CONTINUOUS SURFACE

At Erlangen, Noether studied mathematics mostly with her father and his colleague, Max Gordan. For Gordan she wrote a thesis full of formal manipulations. Later on, she dismissed her thesis as merely "a jungle of formulas," but it was good enough to earn her a mathematics doctorate with highest honors.

"Frl. Noether is continually advising me in my projects . . ."
- Albert Einstein

For the next eight years, Emmy lived at home, working at the university without pay or any formal position. Her father's health was declining, and as he eventually became wheelchair bound, she took over some of his classes. She published papers, gave talks abroad, and supervised doctoral students. Her reputation grew. In 1916, David Hilbert and Felix Klein invited her back to Göttingen to work with them on the mathematics of Einstein's general theory of relativity. As Hilbert said, "Physics is much too hard for physicists." Eager to help, Emmy made the move. Shortly, Einstein was writing to Hilbert, "Frl. Noether is continually advising me in my projects. . . . it is really through her that I have become competent in the subject."

In 1918, Noether proved two theorems that provided a foundation for both general relativity and particle physics. One, which became known as Noether's Theorem, showed the link between symmetry and laws of conservation. Noether's Theorem proves that the laws of physics hold true in any time and place.

All through this period, Noether was still working without pay, supported by a small trust fund established by her uncles. She dressed unconventionally, favoring short hair, a long black coat like a priest's cassock, and a bag slung crosswise across her chest. Because she was allowed no official role, she gave courses that were listed under Hilbert's name. Only in 1919, through the intercession of Einstein and Hilbert, was she finally allowed to lecture under her own name. Still, in 1920, her colleague Hermann Weyl wrote, "I am ashamed to occupy such a preferred position beside Emmy, whom I know to be my superior." At last, in 1922, at age forty, she was made an "associate professor without tenure" and began to receive a small salary. With four strikes against her, as a woman, a Jew, a socialist, and a pacifist, she could hardly expect more.

During the 1920s, Noether turned her mathematical research in new directions. She helped to found the field of abstract algebra, and also worked in group theory, ring theory, and number theory. Dealing in abstractions, she stripped numbers and examples from her thinking, working instead

EMMY NOETHER LECTURING

with pure concepts. By doing so, she was able to bring together questions in algebra, geometry, and topology that other mathematicians had considered quite different. Her nephew Herman Noether wrote that she pursued math "for the fun and intellectual interest of it. If she knew how useful her mathematics had become today, she'd probably turn over in her grave."

In Göttingen, as one of only two women professors in a faculty of 237, Emmy fit in as "one of the boys," frank, loud, and cheerful. She was the lowest-paid professor at the university, but she didn't seem to have much need for money: she helped support her youngest brother and saved for her nephews' education. She also shared food and belongings with her "boys," the students she mentored. She claimed no particular ownership of ideas, and happily encouraged students to develop her ideas into papers and theses of their own. She loved to walk and talk loudly at the same time, to swim in the public pool under the "Men Only" sign, and to eat at the same cheap restaurant six days a week.

Students, including foreign students, swarmed to Noether's classes. Rather than formal lectures, these tended to be spontaneous conversations emanating from students' mathematical ideas. Many of her students went on to become important mathematicians, working in such areas as ring theory and group theory.

Noether spent a year as a visiting professor in Moscow and several months teaching in Frankfurt. In 1932, she became the first woman invited to lecture to a plenary session of the International

MATHEMATICS

Congress of Mathematics. That year she also won the prestigious Ackerman-Teubner Memorial mathematics prize for work in mathematical analysis. She had forty-five publications and an international reputation; she could reasonably expect another twenty years of creative contributions.

Then Adolf Hitler was elected German Chancellor. For some time, Nazism had been growing popular among university students, who wore swastikas and the brown shirts of Hitler's storm troopers to class. Soon the education ministry began firing Jewish professors. At Göttingen, Emmy Noether showed up on the first list of professors to be dismissed. Her students and colleagues rallied to her side, petitioning the education ministry to reinstate her on the grounds that all her students, and even her mathematical ideas themselves, were "Aryan."

The petitioners were unsuccessful. After all, Noether was not only a Jew, but also a woman and a socialist. Hitler pronounced, "Woman's world is her husband, her family, her children and her home. We do not find it right when she presses into the world of men." He had made a campaign promise to remove 800,000 women from the work force, presumably to open their jobs to men.

Instead of lamenting her loss, Noether simply began offering seminars in her apartment. The same students attended as before. When one showed up in his storm trooper's uniform, she just laughed and let him enter. As her friend Hermann Weyl said of her later, "Her courage, her frankness, her unconcern about her own fate, her conciliatory spirit, were, in the midst of all the hatred and meanness, despair, and sorrow . . . a moral solace."

Alarmed on her behalf, Noether's friends began seeking a post for her abroad. The best offer came from Bryn Mawr, a women's college in Pennsylvania, which offered a one-year position with a $4000 salary. Noether took up her new duties in the fall of 1933. Urged by her women friends to dress appropriately, she turned in her favorite beret for a more conventional hat—but tossed it aside as soon as she saw hatless women on campus.

---

*Pioneers of **abstract algebra** sought to examine the structures and rules of algebra that are more fundamental than the problems, numbers, and calculations familiar to us. The building block of abstract algebra is the set, a group of elements. A group is a set that obeys certain rules when you apply an operation (which could be adding, multiplying, or something much less familiar) between any two members of the set. The resulting product must also be a member of the original set.*

Below is an example of the multiplication table for a very simple set that contains only two elements, 1 and a. The key rule that makes this set a cyclic group is that a * a = 1.

*	a	1
a	1	a
1	a	1

Read:
a * a = 1   1 * a = a
a * 1 = a   1 * 1 = 1
All solutions to multiplication within the group are members of the group.

Always sociable, Emmy quickly made friends with Bryn Mawr mathematician Anna Pell Wheeler, who had studied at Göttingen. Emmy took on three advanced students and taught them abstract algebra. Mrs. Wheeler warned the students to be kind to Noether, and never to make fun of her despite her thick glasses, clunky shoes, and unfashionable dresses. There was no need. The students loved her. One wrote, "From our point of view, she was one of us, almost as if she too were thinking about the theorems for the first time." Noether took her students on long hikes and even slipped them money when they were in need.

Once a week Noether traveled to Princeton to lecture at the Institute for Advanced Study. There she ran into Einstein and updated him on news from their mutual friends in Germany. With her friend Hermann Weyl, Noether founded the German Mathematicians' Relief Fund, which asked mathematicians who had found jobs abroad to donate one to four percent of their salary to assist new arrivals and those still trying to leave Germany. The amounts distributed by the fund were small but in some cases vital, and Noether remained one of its most generous donors until her death.

In her second year in America, Noether became more troubled. It was clear to her that there would never again be a place for her in Germany, and teaching undergraduates was not enough to stimulate her. With so many Jewish academic refugees, permanent jobs were hard to find. Then, too, she was troubled by a large ovarian tumor that made her look pregnant and weighed her down.

On April 19, 1935, Noether entered the hospital for surgery. Doctors removed a tumor the size of a cantaloupe. At first all went well. But on the fourth day of recovery, Noether's temperature spiked to 109. She lost consciousness and could not be revived. At the age of fifty-three, Emmy Noether, mathematician and exile, was dead. Albert Einstein's letter to *The New York Times* lamented, "Fraulein Noether was the most significant creative mathematical genius thus far produced since the higher education of women began."

NAZI MOTHERHOOD STAMP

Hitler had strong ideas about the role of women in German society: their only real duty was motherhood. He wrote, "The granting of equal rights to women, as demanded by Marxism, does not confer equal rights at all, but constitutes a deprivation of rights, since it draws women into realms of society where they are inferior."

EMMY NOETHER AT BRYN MAWR

BRYN MAWR ENTRANCE

MATHEMATICS

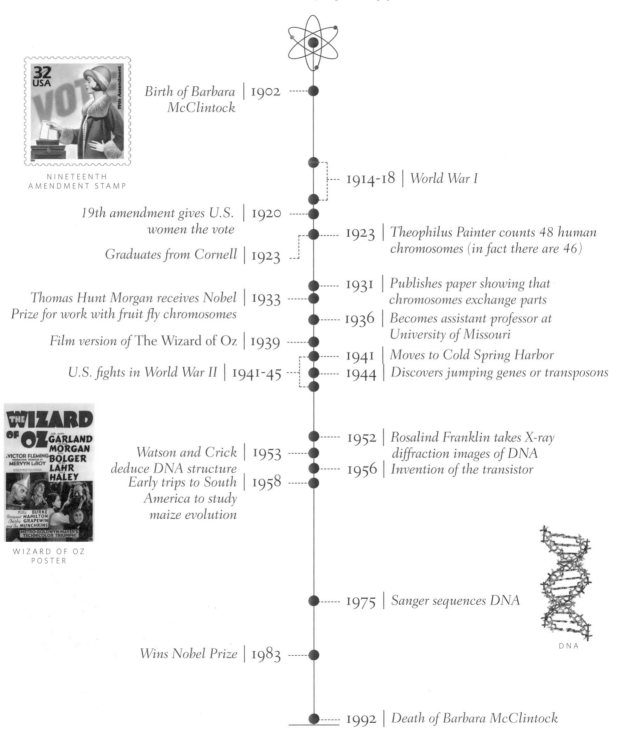

Timeline | 1902-1992

Birth of Barbara McClintock | 1902

NINETEENTH
AMENDMENT STAMP

1914-18 | *World War I*

19th amendment gives U.S. women the vote | 1920

1923 | *Theophilus Painter counts 48 human chromosomes (in fact there are 46)*

Graduates from Cornell | 1923

1931 | *Publishes paper showing that chromosomes exchange parts*

Thomas Hunt Morgan receives Nobel Prize for work with fruit fly chromosomes | 1933

1936 | *Becomes assistant professor at University of Missouri*

Film version of The Wizard of Oz | 1939

1941 | *Moves to Cold Spring Harbor*

U.S. fights in World War II | 1941-45

1944 | *Discovers jumping genes or transposons*

1952 | *Rosalind Franklin takes X-ray diffraction images of DNA*

Watson and Crick deduce DNA structure | 1953

1956 | *Invention of the transistor*

Early trips to South America to study maize evolution | 1958

WIZARD OF OZ
POSTER

1975 | *Sanger sequences DNA*

DNA

Wins Nobel Prize | 1983

1992 | *Death of Barbara McClintock*

12 | *Jumping Genes*

Barbara McClintock

1902-1992 | *United States*

I n 1929, Barbara McClintock puzzled over a cob of multicolored corn, or maize. The pattern of colors in the kernels didn't make sense according to the accepted rules of genetics. But then, in a flash of insight, McClintock thought she knew why. She grabbed a pen and the closest writing surface at hand. On a brown paper bag used to cover tassels of corn in the field, McClintock scrawled the ideas that led to two major papers and eventually a Nobel Prize.

Barbara McClintock was a tomboy. At birth, her parents named her Eleanor, but by the time four months had passed, they decided Eleanor was too soft a name for their little girl. They changed her name to Barbara because it sounded tougher. When Barbara was four years old, her father gave her boxing gloves.

MAIZE

The young tomboy ice-skated, rode a bicycle, and played baseball with the local boys. When her own baseball team was too embarrassed to let her play in an away game because she was a girl, she joined the other team as catcher and helped them win. Convention was never going to keep Barbara McClintock from what she knew she could do.

Barbara graduated from high school during World War I. Her father, a homeopathic physician, was with the army in France, working in the medical corps. Barbara wanted to attend Cornell University, but her mother refused to let her. Too much education, Mrs. McClintock felt, would drive away potential husbands. She had already made Barbara's older sister turn down a scholarship to Vassar. So Barbara took a job in an employment agency and spent her free time in the public library, studying.

As soon as her father returned home, he took his daughter's side. Barbara enrolled in Cornell's free College of Agriculture, becoming the only one of her parents' four children to attend college.

Barbara thrived at Cornell. She became president of the freshmen women, and she played tenor banjo with a jazz band. She smoked, kept her hair very short, and wore golf knickers fastened just below the knee for her fieldwork. She learned Yiddish because her best friends were Jewish women. She took a course in genetics, which fascinated her, but since women were not allowed to major in genetics, she majored in botany instead.

When McClintock graduated from Cornell in 1923, she slipped easily into graduate studies. In the 1920s, perhaps because of the recent war, thirty to forty percent of graduate students in the U.S. were women. Women were well represented in biology, especially in botany. McClintock joined a Cornell group studying the genetics of maize.

YOUNG BARBARA MCCLINTOCK

Genetics is the study of how inherited traits are passed from parental organisms to their offspring. In the 1920s, the notion of a gene was an abstract concept with no physical model. An understanding of DNA's structure was three decades away. Chromosomes, however, had been observed in the nucleus of the cell, and they were known to determine hereditary traits. At Columbia University, the geneticist Thomas Hunt Morgan was studying fruit fly chromosomes. Morgan identified the fruit flies' four chromosome pairs under the microscope, and he "mapped" traits to chromosomes, showing that certain traits, like body color or wing length, tended to be inherited together. These traits mapped onto the same chromosome.

To Barbara McClintock, maize provided a fascinating new model species for studying genetics. For one thing, the pattern of kernels on the multicolored cob was like a chart of its genes. Secondly, each maize plant produces both male and female flowers, so a plant can either be bred to itself or bred with a different specimen. Ordinarily, wind fertilizes maize by blowing male pollen from the tassel at the top of one plant to the female flowers on the cobs of another plant. To control this promiscuous mating, researchers covered the ears of the maize with paper bags and transferred the pollen by hand.

McClintock worked in the botany department staining and examining corn chromosomes under a microscope. No one had studied these chromosomes before. McClintock was able to map visible traits to chromosomes just as Morgan had done for fruit flies. She worked day and night, nurturing her corn through drought and flood and then spending long hours in the laboratory. By the time she received her PhD at the age of twenty-five, she was already the leader of a group of young Cornell geneticists who remained friends and collaborators throughout their lives. Around the same time, though,

FRUIT FLY

McClintock decided she would never marry. "Marriage would have been a disaster. . . . I knew I was a dominant person. . . . [Men are] not decisive. They may be very sweet and gentle, and I knew that I'd become very intolerant and . . . make their lives miserable."

Immersing herself in her work, McClintock began a series of important papers in maize genetics. In 1929, she suggested a thesis topic to a graduate student named Harriet Creighton. They decided to investigate two physical traits—waxy kernels and purple kernels—that were inherited together on the ninth chromosome. McClintock wanted to show that sometimes chromosomes broke and mended themselves in ways that created new combinations of traits.

Carefully, the two women bred waxy, purple corn with not-waxy, not-purple corn. The next fall, they harvested the ears. Most had kernels that matched one of the two parent strains. But some ears were different. They had either purple kernels that were not waxy or waxy kernels that were not purple. When McClintock and Creighton examined the chromosomes of these odd kernels, they saw that the actual form of the ninth chromosome had changed, with lengths broken off and exchanged between chromosome pairs.

The discovery was huge. Thomas Hunt Morgan heard about it on a visit to Cornell, and he helped the two women publish their paper in August 1931. People called it one of the great experiments of biology, and more than one geneticist said the discovery merited a Nobel Prize.

But in 1931, despite her growing reputation, Barbara McClintock left Cornell. The faculty had made it clear that they would never dedicate a permanent faculty appointment to a woman. For the next five years, McClintock worked in a series of short-term fellowships. "I couldn't wait to get to the laboratory in the morning," she said, "and I just hated sleeping." She treasured the fellowships for the freedom they offered her.

During this time, McClintock began to study how X-rays increased the mutation rate in corn, as they did in fruit flies. She found that X-rays caused chromosomes to break. Sometimes the frayed end of one chromosome found the frayed end of a different chromosome, and the two chromo-

*In 1890, the Brooklyn Museum founded a biological laboratory for the education of high school and college teachers near the town of **Cold Spring Harbor** on the north shore of Long Island. In 1904, the Carnegie Institution began eighty years of funding for genetics and "experimental evolution" research at the lab, now called the Cold Spring Harbor Laboratory.*

*Early work done at the **Cold Spring Harbor Laboratory** included research on eugenics, which has since been discredited. Among the many important discoveries made at the laboratory were the development of hybrid corn, the discovery of a genetic component to cancer, and the discovery and isolation of two human hormones. It was at the Cold Spring Harbor Laboratory that James Watson gave his first public lecture on the structure of DNA in 1953.*

somes healed onto each other, creating new combinations of traits.

In 1931, McClintock became the first woman to do a postdoctoral fellowship at Caltech, although as a woman she was not allowed inside the faculty club. While at Caltech she discovered the nucleolar organizer region of the chromosome. Two years later, in 1933, McClintock used a Guggenheim fellowship to work for six months in Germany. Politics, thyroid problems, loneliness, and the persecution of Jews drove her home early.

> *"Everyone was scared of her."*
> — Helen Crouse, a student

In 1936, at the age of 34, McClintock finally obtained a faculty position at the University of Missouri. But she was only an assistant professor, and her position was insecure. As a lecturer, she spoke so fast she was hard for some students to follow. As a research mentor, she was tough and demanding. "Everyone was scared of her," said one student, Helen Crouse. "You had to have a pretty sturdy constitution to survive."

By 1941, McClintock realized that the university was a dead end for her. Fellow faculty excluded her from department meetings, and administrators were reluctant to accommodate her research. Finally she asked Missouri's dean if she would ever get promoted to a permanent position. He told her no. If her department chair ever left, the dean added, she would probably be fired. Furious, McClintock took an immediate leave of absence, determined never to return to a university.

Still, she needed a place to plant her corn, and she asked her old friend Marcus Rhoades for help. He found her a temporary post at Cold Spring Harbor, a center for the study of evolution on rural Long Island. Within a year, the Carnegie Institution gave Barbara McClintock a permanent research position there. Now she could do research surrounded by geneticists and without the dis-

BARBARA MCCLINTOCK AT COLD SPRING HARBOR

traction of teaching. She wore blue jeans and worked 70 or 80 hours a week. And she kept planting corn.

In 1945, McClintock discovered that when corn chromosomes had broken and reattached several times, one cell would sometimes completely lose a chunk of genetic material that then showed up on another cell. She discovered that chromosomes include switches that turn genes on and off and activators that can make the switch jump around the chromosome. Nowadays, the moving chromosome parts are called *transposons* or *jumping genes*.

Geneticists respected the care and thoroughness of McClintock's work, but scientists in the emerging field of molecular biology did not take her ideas seriously. "I don't want to hear a thing about what you're doing. It may be interesting, but I understand it's kind of mad," one scientist

Two methods of transposition:

1. Cut-and-paste mechanism

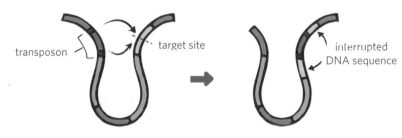

2. Copy-and-paste mechanism

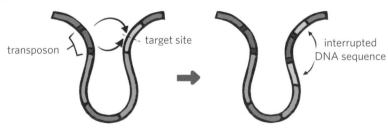

TRANSPOSONS

told her. McClintock's maize genetics was too complicated. Biologists wanted their genes stable, like beads on a chromosome necklace.

Disappointed that so few scientists understood her research, McClintock decided to spend less time reporting it publicly. She nevertheless kept recording and analyzing her results, which she summarized in short notices for the Carnegie Institution year after year. The media portrayed her as something of a recluse, someone difficult and eccentric. But McClintock enjoyed close friendships. She ran, swam, played tennis, and enjoyed long nature walks on Long Island.

Beginning in the late 1950s, the National Science Foundation and Rockefeller Foundation sponsored McClintock on regular trips to South America to study the origins and evolutionary history of maize. She worked with, trained, and advised young scientists from all over the continent, and made a fundamental contribution to the new field of paleobotany.

BARBARA MCCLINTOCK

By the 1960s, molecular biology began to catch up with McClintock. Her work made its way into genetics classes. Scientists discovered transposons in bacteria and even in humans. From the 1960s on, McClintock began accumulating prestigious research awards, including the Albert Lasker Prize, the Wolf Prize, and a MacArthur Fellowship, all during one year, 1980-1981. The awards made her uncomfortable. "I don't like publicity at all," she said.

Then in 1983, at the age of eighty-one, Barbara McClintock heard on the radio that she had won the Nobel Prize for Medicine and Physiology. Marcus Rhoades, in nominating McClintock for the Prize, wrote of her "surpassingly beautiful investigations." Rhoades went on to say,

> *Without technical help of any kind, she has by virtue of her boundless energy, her complete devotion to science, her originality and ingenuity, and her quick and high intelligence made a series of significant discoveries unparalleled in the history of cytogenetics.*

The Nobel Prize, awarded "for her discovery of mobile genetic elements," demonstrated that the world finally understood how McClintock's studies in corn clarified underlying principles of genetics that held true throughout the plant and animal kingdoms.

"Surpassingly beautiful investigations . . ."
— Marcus Rhoades

Although she had officially retired from the Carnegie Institute at age sixty-five, Barbara McClintock continued her research at Cold Spring Harbor through her eighties. She stopped running for exercise and took up aerobics instead. She cut the length of her workday down to eight or nine hours. Some people said she mellowed a bit and became less impatient. She advocated for women in science and kept up her correspondence with colleagues. Still in love with science, she kept reading, traveling, and planning experiments until her death in 1992 at the age of ninety. Her life had been one of incredible focus and discipline, and it had paid off in remarkable discoveries about how genetics and evolution lead to great diversity. Above all, she told interviewers, it had been "a very, very satisfying and interesting life."

Timeline | 1906-1992

Birth of Grace Murray | 1906

19th amendment gives U.S. | 1920
women the right to vote

1928 | Graduates
from Vassar in
mathematics
and physics

Receives PhD in mathematics | 1934

TRANSISTOR

Joins the WAVES | 1943
Begins work on Mark I | 1944

1941-45 | U.S. in World War II

1947 | Brattain and Bardeen
invent the transistor

Creates first compiler | 1952

First dot matrix printer | 1957

1958 | Kilby and Noyce invent the
integrated circuit

WAVES

1975 | Microsoft
founded

ROBERT NOYCE WITH
IC DIAGRAM

NATIONAL MEDAL
OF TECHNOLOGY

Retires with the rank of rear admiral | 1986

1989 | Berners-Lee invents the World
Wide Web

Receives National Medal of Technology | 1991

1992 | Death of Grace Murray Hopper

13 | *Languages of the Admiral*

Grace Murray Hopper

1906-1992 | *United States*

When Rear Admiral "Amazing Grace" Hopper reluctantly retired from the Navy for the last time in 1986, she was the oldest, and probably the smallest, active-duty officer in the service. The inventor of the concept of the computer compiler, she was also recognized as a central figure in the early development of computer programming languages.

Grace Brewster Murray was born in New York City on December 9, 1906. Her father was an insurance broker and her mother an independent woman who loved mathematics. During summers on a lake in New Hampshire, Grace led her younger brother and sister in games of kick-the-can and cops-and-robbers. At home, she liked to read, play the piano, and do needlepoint. She was also curious: at age seven she took apart an alarm clock to find out how it worked. Not

YOUNG GRACE HOPPER

The **U.S. Naval Women's Reserve or WAVES** (Women Accepted for Volunteer Emergency Service) was established as part of the World War II Navy in 1942. Women filled the same ranks and received the same pay as men, though instead of serving on combat ships or aircraft, they worked in the continental United States. In the first year 27,000 WAVES began doing clerical work or serving in communications, intelligence, supplies, or medical care. The first African American WAVES were accepted in 1944.

GRACE HOPPER

sure how to put it back together, she proceeded to disassemble six more clocks before her mother stopped her.

After attending two private schools for girls, Grace applied to Vassar at age sixteen. However, she failed the Latin exam and had to return to high school for another year before enrolling. At Vassar, she majored in mathematics and physics, graduating in 1928 at the age of twenty-one. She pursued further study at Yale University, earning a master's degree in mathematics in 1930 and her PhD in 1934. The year she received her master's degree, she married Vincent Hopper, a professor at New York University, and the following year she began teaching mathematics at Vassar. Although the marriage ended in 1945, Hopper kept her husband's name and never remarried.

At the beginning of World War II, Grace Hopper, by then an associate professor of mathematics, asked for a leave of absence to join the war effort. At thirty-four, she was considered too old, and at 105 pounds, fifteen pounds too light for the Navy, but she persisted in applying, and in 1943 the authorities relented. Hopper enlisted in the Women's Naval Reserve, or WAVES, and was sent to a training camp in Northampton, Massachusetts. Her later advice to young recruits about to enter training was, "If they put you down somewhere with nothing to do, go to sleep—you don't know when you'll get any more." After graduating first in her Midshipman's School training class, Hopper was sent as a newly commissioned lieutenant to join the Bureau of Ships Computation Project at Harvard University.

In July 1944, when Hopper arrived, the Computation Lab, led by Howard Aiken, had just managed to get its new machine, the Mark I, working. Fifty feet long and weighing thirty-five tons, the machine was basically a giant calculator. Aiken greeted Hopper brusquely: "Where have you been?" He gave her one week to learn "how to program the beast and to get a program running." More specifically, Aiken told her to "compute the coefficients of the arctan series by next Thursday." Hopper set to work and soon became the machine's chief programmer.

HOWARD AIKEN

Grace Hopper was the principal author of the first computer manual, a 561-page operations manual for the Mark I. The manual carefully laid out the sequence of arithmetical operations required for a machine to solve numerical problems. Paul Ceruzzi, a noted historian of computing, has called it "the first extended analysis of what is now known as computer programming since Charles Babbage's and Lady Lovelace's writings a century earlier. The instruction sequences . . . are thus among the earliest examples anywhere of digital computer programs."

At the end of the war, Hopper asked to be transferred to the regular Navy, but was once more rejected because of her age. Instead, she remained in the Reserves and declined the offer of a full professorship at Vassar to keep working at the Harvard laboratory. Soon she was programming the Mark II and then the Mark III computer. It was in the Mark II that the first computer "bug" appeared: a moth that short-circuited one of the machine's

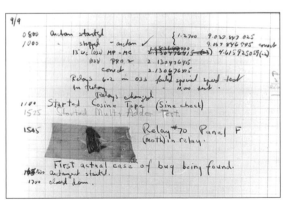

FIRST COMPUTER BUG

relays. When a junior staff member removed the moth, Hopper is reported to have said, "You've debugged the computer." She wrote, "From then on, whenever anything went wrong with a computer,

COMPUTER SCIENCE

> ### *"They told me computers could only do arithmetic."*

we said it had bugs in it." As for the offending moth, its dessicated body can still be seen taped to a page of Hopper's lab notebook at the Computer History Museum in Mountain View, California.

In 1949, Hopper joined a small start-up, the Eckert-Mauchly Computer Corporation, to help develop operating software for the UNIVAC I, the first commercial electronic digital computer. Hopper had a vision that computers would enjoy much wider use if they were only easier to program. She encouraged the UNIVAC programmers to share as much of their programs as possible, and she began to work on a design for a general translator, or compiler. A compiler is a program or set of programs that translate a higher-level computer language or "source code" intelligible to humans into a more fundamental, numbers-based code or "machine language" whose instructions a computer can carry out.

GRACE HOPPER
COURTESY OF THE COMPUTER HISTORY MUSEUM

In 1952, Hopper succeeded in creating the first compiler, which she named "A-o" for automatic programming language zero. Her colleagues were skeptical. Hopper later said, "I had a running compiler and nobody would touch it. They told me computers could only do arithmetic." Hopper began to proselytize for her new vision of computing. As she explained in her landmark article "The Education of a Computer," use of a compiler meant that "the programmer can return to being a mathematician." She went on,

UNIVAC at present has a well grounded mathematical education fully equivalent to that of a college sophomore, and it does not forget and does not make mistakes. It is hoped that its undergraduate course will be completed shortly and it will be accepted as a candidate for a graduate degree.

Hopper's team went on to work on mathematical languages that became the predecessors of FORTRAN. However, her vision was a program that would allow a computer to be programmed entirely in English. She led a team developing the "B-o" language FLOW-MATIC, intended to compile instructions for commercial and business programs. By this time, the Remington Rand Corporation had acquired Eckert-Mauchly, and Hopper's official title was Systems Engineer and Director of Automatic Programming Development of the UNIVAC Division.

Determined to make programming easier and more widely accessible, Hopper began to argue for development of a "Common Business Oriented Language." She actively participated in the first meetings for the effort, served as one of two technical advisers to the Executive Committee, and salted the team with many of her own staff. Since FLOW-MATIC was the leading business application language in the field, it became the foundation for the new language. More than fifty years later, COBOL is still in use throughout the world on virtually every computing platform. Grace Hopper's persistence, technical expertise, and persuasive skills had made her probably the most important contributor to the development of early programming languages.

During her time at Rand Remington and later, after a merger, at the Sperry Corporation, Hopper maintained both her Navy ties and her academic connections. She was a frequent guest lecturer in university courses. In 1966, having reached the Navy's mandatory retirement age of sixty, she left the Naval Reserves bearing the rank of Commander. However, a few months later she was recalled to active duty for a six-month tour that was soon extended indefinitely. She took a leave from Sperry but continued her academic work, lecturing in Management Sciences at George Washington University between 1971 and 1978.

In the navy, Hopper continued to rise in rank, first to captain, then to commodore and finally to rear admiral. Her first active duty assignment was to standardize

COBOL was created to address a problem: programming computers cost too much. Each time a hardware manufacturer built a new computer, or a business bought a new computer, programmers had to be brought in to rewrite all the programs for the new machine, at a cost of hundreds of thousands of dollars. In 1959, a group of academics and computer manufacturers and users convinced the Department of Defense to sponsor an effort to create a common program that could become the standard for business applications. Several committees were formed to examine existing programs and develop specifications for the new common language. The committee agreed that the new language should use English whenever possible, should be easy to improve in future, and should be easy to program even at the expense of speed and power.

In 1960, the first COBOL programs could run on different kinds of computers with only minor modifications. By 1997, COBOL was running 80% of business computer programs worldwide.

COMMODORE GRACE HOPPER

the programming languages used throughout the Navy. The standards she developed eventually became mandatory, not only throughout the Department of Defense, but across the computer industry. In 1977, she was appointed special advisor to the commander of the Naval Data Automation Command. When she finally retired just a few months shy of her eightieth birthday, a celebration was held aboard the USS *Constitution*, the oldest active duty ship in the Navy. At the ceremony, Grace Murray Hopper was awarded the Distinguished Service Medal, the Department of Defense's highest honor.

Restless in retirement, Hopper became a senior consultant to the Digital Equipment Corporation. She represented Digital at industry forums, made presentations on new directions in computing, and served as a liaison to academic institutions. Even after her retirement, she always appeared in full naval uniform. One of her favorite demonstrations concerned the importance of efficiency in programming. To make the concept of a nanosecond more concrete, she held up a piece of wire a foot long, explaining that it represented the distance light could travel in one nanosecond—a billionth of a second. A microsecond would be one thousand times longer. "Don't waste a microsecond!" she urged her programmer audience.

Throughout her career, Hopper received many industry and academic awards, including at least thirty-seven honorary degrees. Among other honors, she became a Fellow of the Institute of Electrical and Electronics Engineers (1962) and of the American Association for the Advancement of Science (1963). In 1969, the Data Processing Management Center, apparently oblivious to the irony, named her the first ever Computer Man of the Year. In 1973 she became the first woman and the first American elected to the British Computer Society. In 1991, in the Rose Garden of the White House, President George H.W. Bush awarded her the National Medal of Technology for

"Humans are allergic to change. They love to say, 'We've always done it this way.' I try to fight that. That's why I have a clock on my wall that runs counter-clockwise." - Grace Murray Hopper

USS *HOPPER*

her fifty-year contribution as a computer pioneer. And in 1997, the Navy commissioned the USS *Hopper* in honor of the admiral who never went to sea.

Grace Hopper's contributions to the early development of computing were fundamental. One of the most important was her early recognition that programming rather than hardware presented the greater barrier to progress in computing technology. The concept of a compiler was hers, and she was the first to demonstrate that a computer language that was easy to understand and use could be translated into machine language whose instructions a computer would obey. Successful in academia, industry, and the military, Hopper demonstrated that there were no limits to what a woman could contribute to the world of computers. The standards she helped develop for the industry remain fundamentally important today.

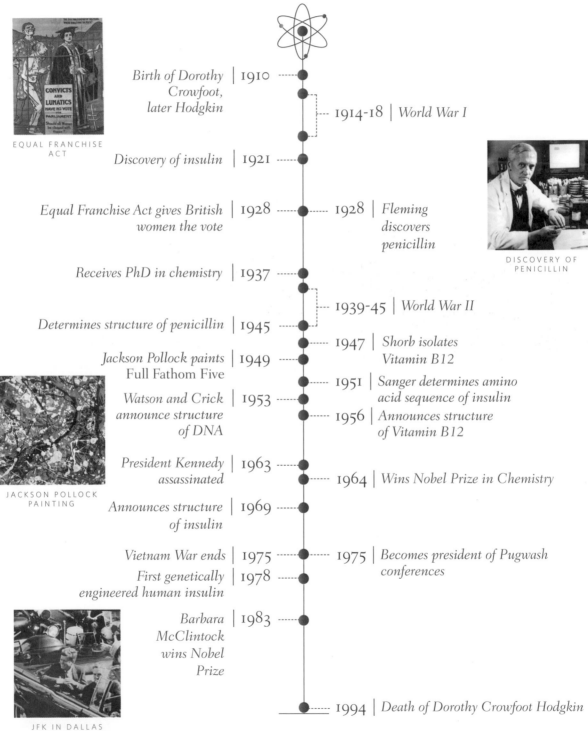

Timeline | 1910-1994

EQUAL FRANCHISE
ACT

Birth of Dorothy | 1910
Crowfoot,
later Hodgkin

1914-18 | World War I

Discovery of insulin | 1921

Equal Franchise Act gives British | 1928
women the vote

1928 | Fleming
discovers
penicillin

DISCOVERY OF
PENICILLIN

Receives PhD in chemistry | 1937

1939-45 | World War II

Determines structure of penicillin | 1945

1947 | Shorb isolates
Vitamin B12

Jackson Pollock paints | 1949
Full Fathom Five

1951 | Sanger determines amino
acid sequence of insulin

Watson and Crick | 1953
announce structure
of DNA

1956 | Announces structure
of Vitamin B12

JACKSON POLLOCK
PAINTING

President Kennedy | 1963
assassinated

1964 | Wins Nobel Prize in Chemistry

Announces structure | 1969
of insulin

Vietnam War ends | 1975

1975 | Becomes president of Pugwash
conferences

First genetically | 1978
engineered human insulin

Barbara | 1983
McClintock
wins Nobel
Prize

1994 | Death of Dorothy Crowfoot Hodgkin

JFK IN DALLAS

14 | *The Mystery of Crystals*

Dorothy Crowfoot Hodgkin

1910-1994 | *England*

One day in 1935, Dorothy Crowfoot, then twenty-five years old, took an X-ray diffraction picture of a crystal of insulin. She shone an X-ray beam through the crystal and onto a photographic plate. That night, after developing the film and seeing a regular diffraction pattern, she wandered through the streets of Oxford, almost delirious with joy at the thought that she might be able to deduce the structure of the molecule so important in treating diabetes. At the time, she had no way of knowing that solving the puzzle would take her thirty-four years.

Dorothy was born in Cairo, Egypt, on May 12, 1910. Her father was an archeologist and educator, and her mother was an expert in ancient weaving who also illustrated texts on botany. Dorothy and her younger sisters spent most of their childhood apart from their parents. Throughout the years of World War I and beyond, the girls stayed with friends or relatives in England while their parents lived mostly in Egypt and Sudan. Both Dorothy's independence and her motherly nature may have grown from those years when she watched over her sisters' welfare.

DOROTHY CROWFOOT HODGKIN

> *"I was captured for life by chemistry and crystals."*
> —Dorothy Crowfoot Hodgkin

Shy, quiet, gentle and independent, Dorothy got a spotty education from a series of small schools. The year she was ten, a government course introduced a project growing crystals. Repeating the experiments at home, Dorothy fell in love with chemistry. Three years later, when she and her sister Joan spent six months with their parents in Sudan, Dorothy prospected for minerals. She enlisted the help of a family friend, soil chemist A.F. Joseph, to analyze them. He gave her a box of reagents, and once Dorothy was home in England again, she set up an attic laboratory for herself. Then, for her sixteenth birthday, her mother gave her a children's book in which physicist William Bragg, winner of the Nobel Prize, described shining X-rays through crystals to discover their atomic structure. Dorothy was captivated by the idea of actually being able to "see" how atoms are arranged.

As a teenager, Dorothy Crowfoot became politically active. Her mother's four brothers had been killed in the world war, and along with her friends, Dorothy joined and volunteered for organizations promoting world peace.

After graduating from high school, Dorothy studied Latin and botany so she could pass the entrance exams to Oxford. At Oxford, studying chemistry, she decided to specialize in the new field of X-ray crystallography. Determining structure from X-ray photographs was harder than Bragg's book had made it sound. First Dorothy had to make crystals of a compound and shine X-rays at them from every angle. Finally she had to analyze the photographs mathematically.

Upon graduating from Oxford, Dorothy joined the laboratory of J.D. Bernal at Cambridge University. Bernal was a Communist, a visionary scientist, and a believer in equal rights for women. His lab was an exciting and sometimes dangerous place to work. Electrical wires hung loose from the ceiling, and there was so much static electricity that Dorothy's hair often stood on end.

While at Cambridge Dorothy began to suffer from swollen, aching joints in her hands. A specialist diagnosed rheumatoid arthritis, a painful, lifelong, and often crippling disease. In the 1930s there was no effective treatment, but Dorothy soldiered on. Her work showed her to be patient, adept, and determined. Her mentor J.D. Bernal said later, "She was one of those masters whose method of work is as exciting and beautiful to follow as the results that flow from it." Handling the samples Bernal's colleagues sent him to study, Dorothy skillfully created X-ray images of vitamins, hormones, and protein crystals.

Even before she received her PhD in 1937, Dorothy Crowfoot received a fellowship at Somerville College, Oxford. That same year, she married Africa scholar Thomas Hodgkin, who like Bernal was an idealist and a Communist. Together they had three children and maintained a warm, chaotic home where international visitors, whether refugees or eminent scholars, came and went with great informality. Thomas did most of the cooking.

OXFORD UNIVERSITY MUSEUM

CHEMISTRY

Despite her marriage, Dorothy Hodgkin found Oxford lonely at first. The university chemistry club did not allow women to attend meetings. Hodgkin's lab was located in the basement of the Oxford University Museum among dinosaur skeletons and medieval stonework. Her equipment was so antiquated she had to convince a senior professor to apply to a chemical firm for funding to buy more. The professor found it hard to turn down a request from the gentle, direct, and well-prepared junior researcher. Asked years later if she felt that being a woman had hindered her career, Dorothy Hodgkin focused her reply on individual kindness rather than institutional barriers. "As a matter of fact," she answered, "men were always particularly nice and helpful to me because I was a woman."

Hodgkin set up her polarizing microscope on a high gallery in front of the sole, high, Gothic window in her basement lab. To reach the microscope, she climbed a ladder, clutching her thin crystal preparation in one arthritic hand and pulling herself up with the other. Then she and her students analyzed their data at a large table in the X-ray room, which bore a sign reading "Danger—60,000 Volts."

Throughout her life, Hodgkin took on challenges in crystallography that others thought were impossible. At Oxford, she began by studying the structure of cholesterol. Although we think of cholesterol mostly in the context of heart disease, it is an essential part of all animal cell membranes.

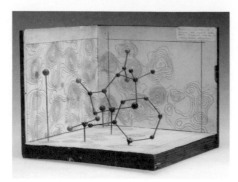

PENICILLIN STRUCTURE

Penicillin *is a chemical secreted when the Penicillium mold is grown under stress. Key to penicillin's structure is a beta-lactam ring. All bacteria have cell walls, which they break down and rebuild as they grow and divide. Beta-lactams prevent the bacteria from forming cross-links in the cell wall. The weakened wall disintegrates, leading to death of the bacteria.*

During World War II, the U.S. mass-produced penicillin by growing mold found on a cantaloupe in deep tanks of a liquid byproduct of corn.

Chemists had already determined its formula—how many atoms of each kind its molecules contained—but not how they were arranged in two or three dimensions. When Hodgkin and her student Harry Carlisle deciphered cholesterol's shape, it was the first time X-ray crystallography had determined a structure that other chemists could not figure out.

In those days, before calculators and computers, solving molecular structures required painstaking calculations with pencil, protractor, and slide rule that could take months or years. But in 1936, Hodgkin spent five pounds on an early version of a calculator: two boxes of paper strips covered in values of sines and cosines for every imaginable X-ray angle. Hodgkin kept the strips carefully organized, and they saved her many hours of figuring.

In 1940, Hodgkin addressed a new challenge—penicillin. Alexander Fleming had discovered penicillin in 1928, but it had to be harvested in small batches from mold cultures. Penicillin was a small enough molecule that Hodgkin thought she could solve its structure. She hoped the structure would allow chemists to synthesize penicillin in large enough amounts to treat Allied soldiers in World War II. But despite its small size, penicillin proved tricky. It crystallized in different arrangements under different conditions. And no one knew what chemical groups made up the molecule. Hodgkin deduced that the heart of the molecule contained a beta-lactam ring, but her colleagues were skeptical. One said, "If penicillin turns out to have the beta-lactam structure, I shall give up chemistry and grow mushrooms."

By the middle of the war, Hodgkin had managed to arrange nighttime use of an early IBM analog computer that tracked ship cargoes during the day. By 1945, she had solved penicillin's structure. For reasons of national security, she did not publish her findings until 1949. But even earlier, her colleagues recognized the scientific quality of her work. In 1946, she was officially appointed an Oxford lecturer and demonstrator. The following year, she became the third woman in almost three hundred years to be elected a fellow of the Royal Society of London.

In 1948, Hodgkin decided to tackle the structure of vitamin B12, also known as cobalamin. People deficient in vitamin B12 cannot make enough blood cells and suffer from neurological problems such as limb weakness, shooting pains, depression, and difficulty thinking. But compared to penicillin's seventeen non-hydrogen atoms, vitamin B12 has nearly a hundred. Most chemists had concluded that the molecule was too complex to solve with X-ray diffraction. Dorothy Hodgkin thought it was worth a try.

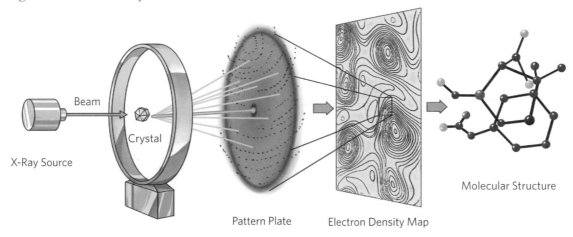

Beam

Crystal

X-Ray Source

Pattern Plate

Electron Density Map

Molecular Structure

CHEMISTRY

X-RAY CRYSTALLOGRAPHY

By now Hodgkin ran a large lab filled with international students, both men and women. She mothered and encouraged them. Together they took thousands of X-ray photographs and gathered mountains of data. Then, in 1953, Hodgkin began collaborating with an American scientist named Kenneth Trueblood, who had helped program an early, high-speed computer to do the calculations needed for crystallography. The computer was housed at UCLA, so Hodgkin and Trueblood communicated by mail or telegraph. In 1956, after eight years of work, Hodgkin announced the structure of vitamin B12. Many chemists considered it the most important structural finding of the decade, just as penicillin had been the decade before.

In the 1950s, although her scientific accomplishments brought her honor, Dorothy Hodgkin's political activities brought her attention of another sort. After World War II ended, she had helped form the International Union of Crystallography. The Union included scientists from East Germany and even the Soviet Union. She also joined a group called Science for Peace that included several Communists. In 1953, Linus Pauling invited her to a conference in California, but the U.S. State Department refused to grant her a visa. Instead of visiting America, Hodgkin traveled to Moscow to discuss ways to improve the exchange of scientific information. In the 1960s and 70s, she continued to work for peace. She opposed the Vietnam War and visited both China and North Vietnam. In 1975 she became president of the Pugwash Conferences on Science and World Affairs, a society established in 1955 to campaign for nuclear disarmament and world peace.

During the Great Depression of the 1930s, Communist ideals of economic fairness attracted many Western intellectuals. During World War II, Stalin's Soviet Union fought with the Allies and helped defeat Hitler's Germany. But relations quickly soured after the war. Spies helped the Soviet Union develop an atomic bomb. The Soviet Union closed Eastern and Central Europe behind the Iron Curtain. Chinese Communists won the Chinese Civil War against the American-backed Nationalist Party. And China backed North Korea against U.S. ally South Korea in the Korean War.

*During the **Red Scare** (1947-1950s), the U.S. government reacted by investigating alleged Communists, requiring loyalty oaths, and scrutinizing visitors. Many prominent scholars were denied visas on the basis of their Communist sympathies or associations.*

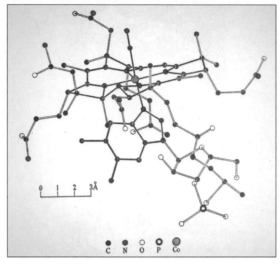

STRUCTURE OF VITAMIN B12, FROM THE ROYAL SOCIETY

Back in Oxford, Hodgkin returned to the insulin puzzle, as she had many times over the years. Insulin regulates sugar uptake and energy use in the body, and lack of it causes the most dangerous form of diabetes. Eight times the size of Vitamin B12, insulin presented a daunting challenge. But in 1951, chemist Fred Sanger identified the sequence of amino acids in the molecule.

DOROTHY CROWFOOT HODGKIN

With computing power rapidly increasing, Hodgkin thought she could decipher the three-dimensional structure at last. To do so, she analyzed thousands of X-ray photographs. In 1969, she and her team announced their solution to the molecule's structure. They showed that insulin consists of six identical sequences arranged in a triangle around two central atoms of zinc.

Throughout the 1950s and 1960s, Thomas Hodgkin had been spending more and more time in Africa. Dorothy was visiting him in Ghana in October 1964 when she learned that she had won the Nobel Prize in Chemistry. In her Nobel biography, she pointed out that at the time of the prize award, her three children were also dispersed across the globe, working in Algeria, Zambia, and India.

"There was magic about her person. She had no enemies . . ."

In 1965, Queen Elizabeth II gave Dorothy Crowfoot Hodgkin the Order of Merit, making her the first woman to receive that honor since Florence Nightingale. In 1977, Hodgkin retired to a stone house in the Cotswolds, north of Oxford. She continued to travel to international conferences on science or peace, despite her crippling arthritis and a broken pelvis. In 1990, she finally received an unrestricted visa to visit America. Although she was over eighty and confined to a wheelchair, Hodgkin immediately scheduled a lecture tour of the U.S. She spoke to standing-room-only crowds about insulin and the history and future of crystallography.

Dorothy Crowfoot Hodgkin died of a stroke in 1994. Her former student M. Vijayan wrote of her: "It is difficult to adequately describe her legendary achievements, but it is still harder to describe her personality in a few words. She was warm, simple, affectionate and caring." Max Perutz, himself a Nobel Prize winner, agreed. "There was magic about her person. She had no enemies, not even among those whose scientific theories she demolished or whose political views she opposed."

Timeline | 1912-1997

Birth of Chien-Shiung Wu | 1912 ----- 1912 | *China becomes a republic under Sun Yat-sen*

SUN YAT-SEN

Graduates from university in Nanjing | 1934 -----

1936 | *Travels to United States*

Japan invades China | 1937 -----

Receives PhD at Berkeley | 1940 -----

Marries Luke Yuan | 1942 ----- 1941-45 | *U.S. in World War II*

Begins work on Manhattan Project | 1944 -----

1945 | *Atomic bombs dropped on Hiroshima and Nagasaki*

Mao Zedong announces | 1949 ----- People's Republic of China

1952 | *Appointed assistant professor of physics at Columbia*

Proves non-parity | 1957 ----- 1957 | *Yang and Lee receive Nobel Prize*
in beta decay

BEATLES IN AMERICA

1962 | *Andy Warhol begins his series of Marilyn Monroe prints*

Beatles visit the | 1964 ----- United States

1965 | *Publishes* Beta Decay

Nixon visits | 1972 ----- China

1975 | *End of Vietnam War*

Death of Mao Zedong | 1976 -----

ANDY WARHOL'S MARILYN MONROE

CHAIRMAN MAO

1997 | *Death of Chien-Shiung Wu*

15 | *Beta Decay*

Chien-Shiung Wu

1912-1997 | *China and the United States*

One day in early spring of 1956, theoretical physicist T.D. Lee climbed to the thirteenth floor of Columbia University's physics lab to consult his colleague Chien-Shiung Wu. Dr. Lee had a problem. He and his partner Dr. Yang wanted to test a new hypothesis that could turn nuclear physics on its head. Up to that time, every interaction observed in physics had been symmetric. That is, every interaction, if seen in a mirror, would look the same. But the idea of symmetry led to some mathematical difficulties when physicists considered the process of radioactive beta decay, in which an atom spontaneously ejects an electron. No one, so far, had been able to show for sure whether beta decay conserved or broke symmetry. So Dr. Lee did what any good theoretical physicist would do: He asked an experimental physicist.

There has always been interplay between theory and experiment in physics. New experimental data may require complete rethinking of theory. Theorists use their imagination and mathematics to pose questions and come up with possible explanations, many of them very difficult to test. Experimentalists use their imagination, skill, and knowledge of measurement to figure out ways to test hypotheses. In this case, Lee and Yang were nearly certain that beta decay would preserve symmetry. But they thought the question should be tested.

Dr. Wu listened to Dr. Lee's questions and made a suggestion. At very low temperatures in a strong magnetic field, she thought it would be possible to detect asymmetric emission of electrons from decaying Cobalt-60, if it occurred. So began a collaboration that led to a Nobel Prize.

Chien-Shiung Wu was born in the town of Liu He, China, not far from Shanghai. The name Chien-Shiung means "courageous hero," and Chien-Shiung's father had great aspirations for her. A former engineer, he believed so strongly in the education of girls that he started China's first

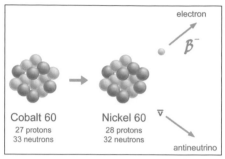

BETA DECAY

Cobalt 60
27 protons
33 neutrons

Nickel 60
28 protons
32 neutrons

electron

antineutrino

Atoms consist of protons and neutrons in a tightly packed nucleus surrounded by clouds or shells of electrons. The number of protons in the nucleus determines the atom's chemical nature – whether it's an atom of gold or of oxygen. But physicists discovered early in the twentieth century that in some cases, an atom of one element can spontaneously transform into an atom of another element, giving off radiation as it does so. Three possible types of radiation—alpha, beta, and gamma—can be emitted during the process.

***Beta radiation** or **beta decay** occurs when an atom spontaneously ejects an electron from its nucleus. With this beta emission, one of the neutrons in the nucleus becomes a proton, changing the atom into a different element with one more proton. For example, an atom of carbon can become an atom of nitrogen. The question Lee and Yang wanted to answer was whether the electrons in beta decay are ejected equally in all directions.*

private girls' elementary school, where he and his wife both taught. But the school went only as far as fourth grade, so at age nine, Chien-Shiung left home for boarding school in the canal-crossed city of Suzhou.

SUZHOU CANAL WITH BOATS

When it came time to choose a course in high school, Soochow Girls' School offered two pathways, an academic track and a Western-oriented course for teacher training. Chien-Shiung chose the teacher track, and although she learned English and enjoyed lectures by visiting American professors, at times she regretted her choice. Girls in the academic track had access to interesting books in chemistry, physics, and mathematics. So at night in their shared dormitory room, Chien-Shiung borrowed and read her schoolmates' books.

In 1930, at the age of seventeen, Chien-Shiung graduated at the top of her high school class. That summer she learned that she had been selected to attend an elite university in Nanjing. She had a crisis of confidence. She knew she wanted to study physics, but she didn't have the right preparation. Luckily, her father stepped in. The day after his daughter's acceptance, he brought home three books, one each of chemistry, physics, and advanced mathematics. "Ignore the obstacles," Principal Wu told his daughter. "Just put your head down and keep walking

"Ignore the obstacles. Just put your head down and keep walking forward."

–Principal Wu, Chien-Shiung's father

forward." Chien-Shiung spent the rest of the summer studying. Years later, she said, "If it hadn't been for my father's encouragement, I would be teaching grade school somewhere in China now."

After graduating from the National Central University in Nanjing in 1934, Wu stayed on as an instructor while doing research in X-ray crystallography. But she wanted to get a PhD, so in1936 she took a ship to the United States. Although she originally intended to study at the University of Michigan, she changed her mind when she learned the university did not allow women in the student union. Wu decided to attend Berkeley instead.

At Berkeley, Wu studied nuclear fission with such great physicists as Ernest Lawrence, who was building the first cyclotron, and Emilio Segre, who later discovered the antiproton. Both men later won Nobel Prizes. J. Robert Oppenheimer, who later directed the Manhattan Project to develop the atomic bomb, also worked at Berkeley. In both her classes and the laboratory, Wu was recognized as an outstanding student. She was elected to Phi Beta Kappa and received her PhD in 1940. But she continued to face barriers because of her sex. In graduate school she missed out on a fellowship, probably because she was Asian and female. After graduation, Berkeley kept her on as a research assistant but did not appoint her to the faculty. At that time, no woman was teaching physics at any major American university.

YOUNG WU

Those years were difficult for another reason as well. In 1937, in the prelude to World War II, Japan invaded China. Wu lost all contact with her family. Only after the war did she learn they were safe. By that time there was civil war in China, and soon after came the Communist takeover. Wu did not return home, and she never saw her family again.

In 1942, Wu married a Berkeley classmate, Dr. Luke C.L. Yuan, and the couple moved east. Yuan got a research position at RCA in Princeton, New Jersey, and Wu taught for a year at Smith College. But by now, with so many men gone for the war, teaching posts suddenly opened up, and Wu received offers from Columbia, Princeton, and MIT. She took a job at Princeton, where she taught nuclear physics to naval officers. Then, in 1944, because of her knowledge of nuclear radiation, Columbia University recruited her to work on war research for the still secret Manhattan Project.

Wu's work focused on improving Geiger counters to better detect radiation. At one point, she helped project leader Enrico Fermi solve a problem that allowed a higher-yield process to enrich uranium.

MAO PROCLAIMS PEOPLE'S
REPUBLIC OF CHINA

*Chien-Shiung Wu's life spanned a tumul-
tuous time in the **modern history of
China.** In 1912, the year of her birth, the
last Chinese emperor abdicated and China
became a republic under Dr. Sun Yat-sen.
But the central government was weak,
and soon a struggle for power erupted
among northern warlords, the Nationalist
Party, and the Communist Party. As World
War II approached, Japan first took over
Manchuria and then invaded China proper
in 1937. The Japanese occupation was
brutal and destructive. In 1941, Japanese
planes bombed Hawaii's Pearl Harbor, and
the United States entered the war.*

*Even after the Allied victory in 1945, peace
did not settle in China. Civil war intensified
between the Nationalist government and
Communist insurgents. The Communists
won. In 1949, Chairman Mao proclaimed
the formation of **the People's Republic
of China.** Forcible redistribution of land,
a series of political purges, and periodic
attacks on intellectuals began.*

After the war, Wu continued as a research associate
at Columbia. In 1947, she and Luke had a son, Vincent,
who also grew up to be a physicist. They moved very close
to the university so that Wu could run back and forth
between her lab and her son. It was probably around this
time that Wu first said, "There is only one thing worse
than coming home from the lab to a sink full of dirty
dishes, and that is not going to the lab at all." In 1952,
Columbia appointed Wu associate professor in physics.
She continued to delve into her specialty, beta decay.

WU AT COLUMBIA

In 1956 and 1957, Wu worked on the experimental challenge Lee and Wang had posed. She enlisted the
low temperature physics lab at the National Bureau of
Standards to help. Together, they used liquid hydrogen
and helium at low pressures to cool Cobalt-60 to 0.01
degree Kelvin, very close to absolute zero. At such a
low temperature, the atoms moved very little. Then the
experimenters magnetized the Cobalt-60 atoms so that
most of their nuclei spun in the same direction. To their
amazement, they showed definitively that nuclei spinning
one way ejected electrons in a different direction from
nuclei spinning the opposite way. Mirror images looked
different. The conservation of parity, or symmetry, until
then thought to be universal in physics, was broken. The

lab team popped the cork on a bottle of champagne. "These are moments of exaltation and ecstasy," Wu recalled later. "A glimpse of this wonder can be the reward of a lifetime."

The news was monumental in the world of physics. Wolfgang Pauli, hearing a report of it, exclaimed, "That's utter nonsense!" But other researchers confirmed the results. One of Wu's Columbia colleagues said, more mildly but with concern, "A rather complete theoretical structure has been shattered at the base, and we are not sure how the pieces will be put together." So important was the discovery that the Nobel committee moved with unusual speed to award the Nobel Prize to Lee and Yang in 1957. To the consternation of many in the physics community, Wu was not included in the prize. Purportedly, the reason was that she had "only" done the experiment to confirm the original ideas of others.

CHIEN-SHIUNG WU

Although extremely disappointed about the Nobel Prize, Wu won a long string of other prizes: the first Wolf Prize from Israel, the first Comstock Prize awarded to a woman, and many others. And she continued her productive line of research. Graduate students sought her out as a research mentor despite her reputation as a "slave driver" who expected them to spend long hours in the lab seven days a week. The awards and honors kept pouring in. Columbia made her a full professor. Princeton awarded her an honorary doctorate, their first ever to a woman in science. She became the seventh woman ever elected to the National Academy of Sciences.

> "*These are moments of exaltation and ecstasy. A glimpse of this wonder can be the reward of a lifetime.*"

In 1963, Wu experimentally confirmed a theory of two later Nobel Prize awardees, Richard Feynman and Murray Gell-Mann. Two years later, she published *Beta Decay*, which became a standard text in nuclear physics. In 1976, the American Physical Society elected her as their first woman president, and that same year President Ford awarded her the National Medal of Science.

After her retirement in 1981, Wu continued to lecture and teach. She spoke up often about barriers to women in science, especially the physical sciences. She even became the first living scientist to have an asteroid named after her.

Chien-Shiung Wu died of a stroke in 1997 at the age of eighty-four. One former colleague said of the small woman from China, "C.S. Wu was one of the giants of physics." As her entry in the National Women's Hall of Fame reads, she had "radically altered modern physical theory and changed our accepted view of the structure of the universe."

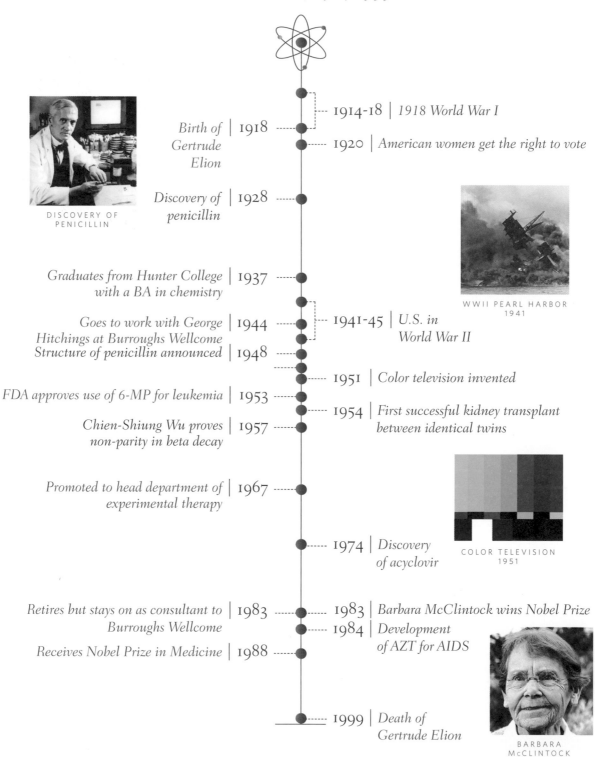

Timeline | 1914-1999

DISCOVERY OF
PENICILLIN

1914-18 | 1918 World War I

Birth of | 1918
Gertrude
Elion

1920 | American women get the right to vote

Discovery of | 1928
penicillin

WWII PEARL HARBOR
1941

Graduates from Hunter College | 1937
with a BA in chemistry

Goes to work with George | 1944
Hitchings at Burroughs Wellcome

1941-45 | U.S. in
World War II

Structure of penicillin announced | 1948

1951 | Color television invented

FDA approves use of 6-MP for leukemia | 1953

1954 | First successful kidney transplant
between identical twins

Chien-Shiung Wu proves | 1957
non-parity in beta decay

Promoted to head department of | 1967
experimental therapy

1974 | Discovery
of acyclovir

COLOR TELEVISION
1951

Retires but stays on as consultant to | 1983
Burroughs Wellcome

1983 | Barbara McClintock wins Nobel Prize

1984 | Development
of AZT for AIDS

Receives Nobel Prize in Medicine | 1988

1999 | Death of
Gertrude Elion

BARBARA
McCLINTOCK

16 | *Inventing Medicines*

Gertrude B. Elion

1918-1999 | *United States*

Gertrude Belle Elion, who became one of the most prolific inventors of new drugs in the twentieth century, was born in New York City in 1918. Her parents, both immigrants, came from families of scholars and rabbis. Her father, Robert, worked as both a dentist and a stockbroker. The family lived in Manhattan until 1929, when the stock market crash led them to move to the Bronx.

Trudy, as she was known, was shy and an outstanding student with no particular interest in science. She skipped two grades and graduated from Walton High School for girls at age fifteen. Luckily, the City College of New York offered qualified applicants a free and excellent college education. When Elion entered Hunter College, the women's branch of CCNY, she was undecided on a major. That changed when her beloved grandfather was hospitalized with stomach cancer. Watching him suffer affected the young college student deeply, and she resolved to study science so she could make a contribution against disease. Four years later, she graduated from college as a member of Phi Beta Kappa with highest honors in chemistry.

Just after graduating, Elion met the love of her life, a statistics student named Leonard Canter. Canter called the redheaded Elion "brilliant . . . a vital, fresh, spon-

GERTRUDE ELION

American women in chemistry: *The first American woman to receive a PhD in chemistry, Rachel Holloway Lloyd, had to study in Switzerland to earn her degree from the University of Zurich in 1878. During the whole of the 1930s, fewer than 300 PhDs in chemistry were awarded to American women. During the first decade of the 21st century, by contrast, about 8300 American women received PhDs in chemistry.*

taneous, sparkling spirit." They dated for four years, attending plays and concerts and discussing science. Canter respected Elion's ambitions. Determined to get a PhD but lacking money, Elion needed financial aid in the form of a graduate fellowship to continue. Unfortunately, despite her academic achievements, fifteen graduate programs in chemistry rejected her, largely because she was female. One university told her, "You're qualified. But we've never had a woman in the laboratory before and we think it would be a distracting influence."

Discouraged, Elion enrolled in secretarial school. Soon, though, she got a better offer: two hundred dollars to teach chemistry to nursing students for three months. She took the post. After some hesitation, she also agreed to volunteer in a chemistry lab at Denver Chemical Company. It meant an exhausting day, riding two and a half hours on the subway, rushing through dinner, hurrying off to teacher training classes, and not getting home until ten o'clock at night. But Elion wrote to Canter, "It's worth it—if only for the feeling of confidence it's giving me."

Then Canter received a scholarship to study in Paris

> *"Nothing worthwhile comes easily. Don't let others discourage you . . ."*

for a year. While he was gone, Elion's volunteer position turned into more: the Denver Chemical Company began paying her a salary. Soon, Elion had saved enough money—$450—to enroll in the graduate chemistry program at New York University. A morning job as a doctor's receptionist and occasional assignments as a substitute teacher helped cover her expenses. Later, Elion would advise young women, "Don't be afraid of hard work. Nothing worthwhile comes easily. Don't let others discourage you or tell you that you can't do it. In my day I was told women didn't go into chemistry. I saw no reason why we couldn't."

When Canter returned from Paris, he graduated from college with a strong academic record, but he, too, had difficulty finding work. He lost a job offer at Macy's when the company doctor discovered he had a "heart condition," perhaps rheumatic heart disease. Canter was devastated, but not long afterward he found a job at a stock brokerage. He and Elion became engaged. Then, in November of that year, Canter fell ill with bacterial endocarditis, an infection of the heart valves. Without penicillin, which was not yet available, the disease was incurable. After more than six months of illness, with Elion at his side, Canter died. Elion wrote that he took with him "faith, hope, consolation, beauty." For many years afterward, Elion did not date; she never married. Work became everything to her. She later explained that she believed marriage wasn't an option for a woman who wanted a serious career in the science. "If a woman got married, she was often fired; if she had a child, no question—out she'd go. There was no such thing as maternity leave." After Canter's death, Elion rededicated herself to her goal: harnessing chemistry to cure illness.

Four years later, World War II arrived, pulling so many men out of the labor market that opportunities for women blossomed at last. "I don't know if I would ever have gotten into a research lab without the men being gone," Elion later reflected. The A&P grocery chain hired her as a quality control officer testing food products. It was chemistry, if only of a very simple kind. Elion checked strawberries for mold, measured the pH of pickle juice, and assessed how egg yolks colored the mayonnaise. She also learned about quality control.

In 1944, Johnson & Johnson invited her to join a small research lab to help develop sulfa drugs. Here at last was her chance to make a real difference. But the new lab closed after only six months, and when J&J asked her to start testing the strength of surgical thread instead, Elion decided it was time to move again.

This time her dentist father gave her the lead. He had received a free sample of Empirin, a codeine-aspirin mix, from the pharmaceutical company Burroughs Wellcome. Why not try there for a research position? Elion did, and George Hitchings hired her for fifty dollars a week. Elion told herself she would stay only as long as she kept learning. She stayed nearly forty years, learning organic chemistry, biochemistry, microbiology, cancer medicine, immunology, and virology. At first she continued to take night courses toward a PhD at Brooklyn Polytechnic Institute. Eventually, though, the university gave her a choice: drop her job and attend full time or leave the PhD program. Elion chose the job.

Thirteen years older than Elion, with a Harvard PhD in biochemistry, Hitchings had been working at Burroughs Wellcome for two years as the company's sole biochemist. Elion's arrival in 1944 marked the beginning of thirty years of remarkably productive collaboration. Most drugs throughout history had been discovered either accidentally or by trial and error, but George Hitchings had a different idea. With enough understanding of biochemical processes, he thought, drugs could be designed more rationally.

When Elion joined the lab in 1944, Hitchings was pursuing an interest in nucleic acids, the building blocks of DNA. Just that year, Oswald Avery had published evidence that DNA is the molecule that carries genetic information. The actual structure of DNA would not be worked out by Watson, Crick, and Franklin for another nine years. But Hitchings and Elion reasoned that bacteria and tumor cells, which grow much faster than healthy human cells, would need to build a lot of DNA. Therefore, interfering with DNA synthesis might be a rational approach to attacking cancer or infection.

Hitchings assigned Elion to investigate the class of nucleic acids known as purines. She spent long hours in the library and in the laboratory learning how to synthesize these molecules. If she could design molecules similar to naturally occurring purines, and if these analogs latched onto the enzymes involved in DNA synthesis, then, like the wrong key jammed in a lock, they might physically block the enzymes from working on the actual purines needed to build DNA. Thus, the new compounds might block the kind of fast cell growth that happens in bacteria or tumors. This class of drugs came to be known as **antimetabolites** because they interfere with the normal growth and workings, or metabolism, of a cell.

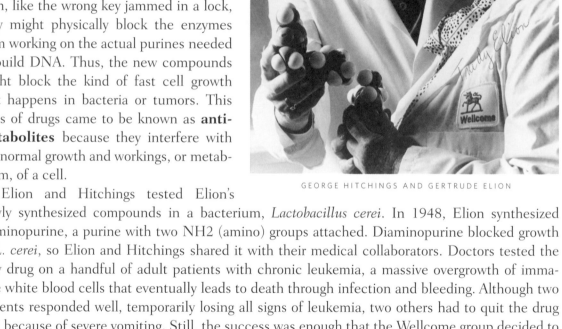

GEORGE HITCHINGS AND GERTRUDE ELION

Elion and Hitchings tested Elion's newly synthesized compounds in a bacterium, *Lactobacillus cerei*. In 1948, Elion synthesized diaminopurine, a purine with two NH2 (amino) groups attached. Diaminopurine blocked growth in *L. cerei*, so Elion and Hitchings shared it with their medical collaborators. Doctors tested the new drug on a handful of adult patients with chronic leukemia, a massive overgrowth of immature white blood cells that eventually leads to death through infection and bleeding. Although two patients responded well, temporarily losing all signs of leukemia, two others had to quit the drug trial because of severe vomiting. Still, the success was enough that the Wellcome group decided to focus the majority of their efforts on cancer.

Next Elion tried substituting a sulfur atom for an oxygen atom on a purine molecule, creating 6-mercaptopurine or 6-MP. Here was a drug that routinely sent acute leukemia in children into remission, increasing the average survival after diagnosis from just a few months to a year or more.

> *Today almost 80 percent of childhood leukemia victims can be cured.*

Still, all the patients eventually relapsed, an outcome Elion found so heartbreaking that she spent the next six years working to understand everything about how 6-MP worked. She learned that combining 6-MP with other drugs led to longer remissions, sometimes permanent ones. Today, using combination chemotherapy including 6-MP, almost 80 percent of childhood leukemia victims can be cured.

During this period, Elion wrote a number of papers with herself listed as first author. Hitchings appeared as senior author, indicating that the work had been done in his laboratory under his general direction. Hitchings trusted Elion's instincts and her productivity, so he tended to give her free rein to follow the directions she chose in her research. It worked well. Elion eventually filed forty-five patents for new drugs.

Using the same principles of rational design that had worked so well for 6-MP, Elion went on to develop other drugs. When she synthesized a related compound called 6-thioguanine, she found that not only did it reduce white blood cell overgrowth, it also seemed to blunt the body's immune response. At that time, surgeons were beginning to experiment with organ transplant for such problems as kidney failure. The problem with transplanted organs was that unless the donor and recipient were identical twins, the recipient's body "saw" the transplanted organ as a foreign body and sent white blood cells to reject and destroy it. Elion shared 6-TG with researchers at the Peter Bent Brigham Hospital in Boston, who found that dogs treated with the drug would accept a transplanted kidney.

The Wellcome team extended and refined their work on 6-TG to discover a new compound, azathioprine. Under the trade name Imuran, the compound successfully suppressed the body's tendency to reject newly transplanted organs. Azathioprine also effectively treated the painful and crippling disease rheumatoid arthritis.

The team's remarkable productivity persisted. They developed allopurinol, a drug that decreases the production of uric acid. At high levels in the blood, uric acid can form crystals in joints, causing the painful form of arthri-

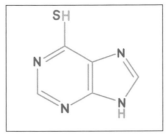

6-THIOGUANINE

6-MERCAPTOPURINE

ALLOPURINOL

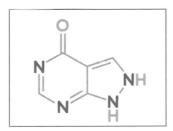

ACYCLOVIR

AZT

CHEMISTRY

*The **herpesviruses** are a family of DNA-containing viruses that cause a range of human diseases, including cold sores, genital sores, chickenpox, shingles, and mononucleosis, sometimes called "kissing disease." Their name comes from the Greek word **herpein**, meaning "creeping," because the infection often flares and then becomes latent, hiding in a blood cell or nerve root until it flares again. Some kinds of herpes infections can spread to the brain, lungs, or eyes, leading to disability or death. Chickenpox, for example, is especially dangerous in pregnant women or people whose immune systems are not working properly; shingles involving the eye can cause blindness.*

Acyclovir is useful in most of these conditions. It works by blocking a version of an enzyme used in assembling DNA that is only found in herpesviruses.

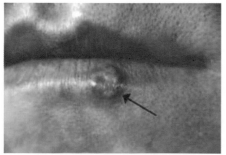

ACYCLOVIR, ACTIVE AGAINST HERPES

HERPES COLD SORE

tis called gout, or in the kidney, causing kidney stones that can lead to kidney failure. They developed a new drug against malaria called pyrimethamine and a new drug against bacterial infections called trimethoprim.

In 1967, as a result of this stunning run of successes,

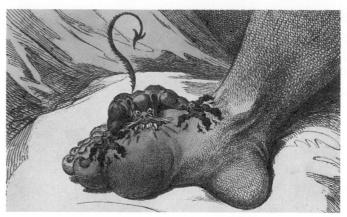

GOUT, CARTOON BY JAMES GILLRAY, 1799

Hitchings was promoted to vice president for research at Burroughs Wellcome. The new position meant that he no longer did bench research, and Elion was promoted to head the department of experimental therapy. For years Elion and Hitchings had collaborated closely, publishing papers and filing patents together. Now she was running her own lab, with no break in the flow of invention.

Elion returned to a longstanding interest, asking whether compounds could be found to treat viral infections. When Howard Schaeffer synthesized a new drug, acyclovir, Elion focused on finding out exactly what it did and how it worked. She discovered that the drug works selectively to inhibit replication of DNA in the herpes virus. Marketed as Zovirax, acyclovir became a mainstay of treatment for genital and oral herpes as well as life-threatening conditions such as herpes encephalitis, or herpes infection of the brain. Elion called acyclovir "my crown jewel," and it became Burroughs Wellcome's best-selling product. Even more importantly, their success with herpes convinced the Burroughs Wellcome team that they could develop drugs against specific viruses. Later, a team Elion had trained synthesized azidothymidine, better known as AZT, the first drug effective against HIV and the first specific treatment for people with AIDS.

In 1970, the Wellcome Laboratory moved from New York to Research Triangle in North Carolina. Elion moved with it. Still lacking a PhD, she became a research professor at Duke University. In 1983, eight years after her mentor Hitchings left Wellcome, Gertrude Elion too officially retired. Although she enjoyed photography, travel, listening to music, and attending the ballet and theater, she also went back to the lab whenever she could.

In her later years, Elion received many honors. Her honorary doctorate from the Polytechnic University of New York was only one of twenty-three honorary degrees. She was elected to the National Academy of Sciences, the Institute of Medicine, and the American Association of Arts and Sciences. She won a National Medal of Science, and she was the first woman inducted into the National Inventors Hall of Fame. In 1988, along with George Hitchings and Sir James Black, she won the Nobel Prize in Physiology and Medicine "for their discoveries of important principles for drug treatment."

"What we were aiming at was getting people well . . ."

Asked once if she had spent her life aiming for the Nobel Prize, Elion answered, "What we were aiming at was getting people well, and the satisfaction of that is much greater than any prize you can get." In a box by her bedside she saved her greatest prizes of all—letters of thanks from patients and the parents of patients cured by her inventions. Curing the sick and relieving suffering had always been her goal, but there was more. At the end of her Nobel lecture, Gertrude Elion reminded her audience, "Chemotherapeutic agents are not only ends in themselves but also serve as tools for unlocking doors and probing Nature's mysteries." As for so many women in this book, Gertrude Elion found that the sheer fascination of scientific discovery brought a joy all its own.

CHEMISTRY

Timeline | 1942-2019

---- 1942 | *Birth of Patricia Bath*

---- 1952 | *Albert Schweitzer awarded
Nobel Peace Prize*

---- 1959 | *Summer research program at
Yeshiva University*

*Assassination of Martin Luther King
and Robert F. Kennedy* | 1968 ------ ----- 1968 | *Bath graduates from medical school*

---- 1974 | *President Nixon resigns*

*Proposes
community
ophthalmology* | 1978 ----

---- 1983 | *Becomes first female director
of an ophthalmology
residency program*

Sabbatical for laser research | 1986 ----

Earns first patent | 1988 ----

---- 1989 | *Berlin Wall falls*

---- 1993 | *Retires from UCLA*

ROBERT KENNEDY

*Barack Obama
elected President* | 2008 ----

BARACK OBAMA

BERLIN WALL

Death of Patricia Bath | 2019 ----

17 | *The Right to Sight*

Patricia Bath

1942-2019 | *United States*

When Patricia Bath was a young girl in Harlem, she never met a woman physician. She admired her family doctor, but her true hero was Albert Schweitzer. She read stories about him in the newspaper: the musician, humanitarian, and physician who founded a hospital and treated people with leprosy on the west coast of Central Africa. In 1952, Schweitzer was awarded a Nobel Peace Prize for living his philosophy of "Reverence for Life." The ten-year-old Bath took his message to heart: all people are equally deserving of health care. This belief motivated her life's work in medicine, leading her to accomplishments as a surgeon and inventor that allowed her to change systems of medical training and care.

ALBERT SCHWEITZER

Patricia Bath was born on November 4, 1942 at Harlem Hospital, just a year after her brother Rupert. Patricia's father, also named Rupert, was an immigrant from Trinidad who had traveled widely in the merchant marine. He loved to tell his children stories of the faraway lands he had visited. Some of these stories worked their way into a weekly column he wrote for a local newspaper. In New York, Rupert found work as a railroad porter, but he knew he could do more. At that time, there were no Black

PATRICIA BATH

In 1960, only 7% of first-year medical students were women, and even by 1968, only 3% of the entering class nationwide was non-white. (Today women make up more than 50% of those entering medical school; 7% of entering students are African American, and 6% are Latino/a.)

motormen, or operators, on any subway train in New York City. Rupert Bath enlisted the NAACP to lobby for him. When he was finally allowed to take the licensing exam, he passed it easily, opening gateways for other African Americans behind him.

Patricia's mother, Gladys, was the descendant of African slaves and Cherokee Indians. She stayed at home to care for her two children when they were small, and later she worked as a domestic servant in fancy Park Avenue homes. "She scrubbed floors to pay for my medical education," Patricia Bath said later.

Although neither of Patricia's parents had more than a high school education, they encouraged their children's learning. Patricia especially remembered her mother giving her a chemistry set, which fed her curiosity. The children were expected to study hard, get high grades, and go to college. The barriers were many. Harlem didn't even have a high school of its own, so the two Bath children attended Charles Evans Hughes High School in Manhattan's Chelsea neighborhood. There they both excelled in math and science. Patricia became the editor of the high school's science newspaper. Her teachers encouraged her to pursue a science career, and in 1959, the sixteen-year-old Bath was chosen for a summer research program at Yeshiva University.

Female, Black, and Christian, Bath stuck out among the mostly white, male, Jewish young scholars in the program. Still, she soon made friends and plunged into a project studying links among nutrition, stress, and cancer—much too big a subject for a summer project! Nevertheless, she developed an equation predicting the growth of cancer cells that one of her mentors, Dr. Robert Barnard, included in a presentation at an international conference the following year. Because of this work, *Mademoiselle* magazine honored Bath as one of ten young women to receive its 1960 Merit Award.

Bath completed high school in two-and-a-half years and went on to major in chemistry and physics at New York's City's then-free Hunter College, which has produced two female Nobelists in medicine. She was

RESURRECTION CITY, POOR PEOPLE'S CAMPAIGN

The Poor People's Campaign *grew out of the Civil Rights movement A month after Martin Luther King's assassination on April 4, 1968, nine caravans of poor people of all races journeyed to Washington, where thousands of them camped in tents on the Washington Mall. They petitioned Congress and government agencies, demanding full employment, universal income, access to land and capital for marginalized people, and a chance for poor people to participate meaningfully in government. After six weeks, the camp was broken up and the people went home with few concrete accomplishments.*

determined to attend medical school, despite obstacles of poverty, sexism and racism. Bath selected Washington, DC's Howard University, whose medical school was founded in 1868, after the Civil War, to train physicians to care for the city's freedmen. It was her first time being exposed to black professors, which she found "electrifying and uplifting." Howard students were trained to take a socially conscious approach to the practice of medicine, and to strive to provide equally high-quality medical care for all races.

Bath spent one of her medical school summers working on a pediatrics research project in Yugoslavia. The experience stirred the travel bug she had inherited from her father. The following summer, 1968, she coordinated medical care and sanitary provisions for the Poor People's Campaign march on Washington. The experience only further strengthened her dedication to providing the same high quality medical care to all people.

Upon graduating from Howard in 1968, Bath returned to New York City for an internship at Harlem Hospital. From there she needed to decide on a residency program and an area of medicine for further training. She chose the difficult and highly specialized field of ophthalmology (eye care and surgery). A pioneer like her father, Bath become the nation's first African American

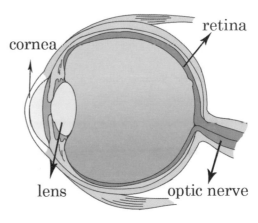

DIAGRAM OF THE EYE

> *"The ability to restore sight is the ultimate reward."*

woman to complete a residency in ophthalmology, first studying at Columbia University's College of Physicians and Surgeons and then finishing at New York University and Harlem Hospital. Bath was struck by the disparities in eye health between the two hospitals: at Harlem Hospital, far more of the patients were blind. In fact, she discovered that glaucoma, in which raised eye pressures lead to blindness, occurred twice as often in Blacks as in whites. Moreover, Harlem Hospital offered no eye surgery. Bath convinced some of her professors at Columbia to come to Harlem to operate on the community's poor blind patients for free, with herself working as assistant surgeon. In 1970, the first eye operations were held at Harlem Hospital.

Around this time, Bath entered a relationship with a charismatic young anesthesiologist at Harlem Hospital named Beny Primm, who later became a noted HIV/AIDS researcher and advocate. Their daughter Eraka was born on February 3, 1972. Bath carried on, completing a fellowship in surgery on the cornea—the clear window lying over the eye's iris—and replacing the lens.

In 1974, Bath and baby Eraka moved to Los Angeles, where Bath became assistant professor of surgery and ophthalmology at both UCLA and the Charles M. Drew University of Medicine and Science, named after the African American pioneer of blood banking. A year later, she was asked to become the first female faculty member at UCLA's Stein Eye Institute. As Bath later said, "I was offered an office in the basement next to the lab animals, which I refused. I didn't say it was racist or it was sexist. I said it was inappropriate." She got a better office and went to work.

Bath was still determined to tackle the inequality in eye care available to different groups of people. She saw no reason why some people should be suffering high rates of preventable blindness, and she thought she had a solution. Because it required years of specialized training, eye surgery had always been available to only a few, but Bath was convinced that many eye problems could be prevented or treated before they needed surgery. She proposed to create a new field of medicine: community ophthalmology, blending the fields of public health, ophthalmology, and community medicine.

The key was training a cadre of eye health care workers, eye health educators, and ophthalmic assistants. Their work would include everything from teaching people in dusty climates about the importance of hand and face-washing to prevent trachoma, to testing vision and providing eyeglasses, to convincing people that loss of sight in old age is not inevitable. Bath wrote a paper about her idea and then, working with psychiatrist Alfred Cannon and pediatrician Aaron Ifekwunigwe, founded the American Institute for the Prevention of Blindness. The Institute urged health workers to use anti-infective eyedrops in newborns. They championed giving Vitamin A supplements to malnourished children, and they pushed for universal vaccination against measles, which is a leading cause of child blindness in the developing world. Bath traveled all over the world, doing surgery, teaching, and promoting her ideas. In 1981 she took her fifth-grade daughter

Eraka with her on a lightning tour to seven countries, including Pakistan, Nigeria, Greece, Italy, France and Thailand, to lecture about community ophthalmology. She kept up her own practice, travel, and research while raising her daughter.

Bath was an involved mother. She and Eraka lived on a cul-de-sac in an upper middle class African American neighborhood, and they ate dinner together every night. The community had a lot of stay-at-home moms keeping an eye on the kids of the neighborhood as they played together. Eraka was a well-behaved and studious girl who preferred the humanities to the sciences. Her mother conveyed high expectations but did not hover or check her homework. After high school, Eraka attended UC Berkeley, where she found herself one of still only a handful of Black or Latino students in science classes. Physics was hard, and no one wanted to be her lab partner, but she pulled through. Following her mother's example, Eraka went to medical school. Eventually, she became a psychiatrist and joined the faculty at the UCLA medical school.

Meanwhile, in 1983, seeking to increase the number of trained ophthalmologists who could treat the poor, Patricia Bath co-founded a residency program in ophthalmology shared between UCLA and Drew. As leader of the program, she became the first female director of any ophthalmology residency in the country. She focused on giving young doctors the same experience treating a diverse population that had inspired her in New York.

Around this same time, in her early forties, Bath began to think there might be a better way to operate on cataracts. Cataracts are cloudy areas in the lens of the eye, and as they grow they can lead to blindness. The most advanced treatment of the day used ultrasound to break up the cataract within the lens, allowing it to be extracted in small pieces. Bath thought a laser, with its intensely focused beam of light at a specific wavelength, might work better, but her colleagues were unconvinced. Although she was respected as a teacher and surgeon, she found as a Black woman that her colleagues could not think of her as an inventor. So she went abroad.

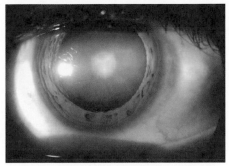

CATARACT IN THE HUMAN EYE

The first cataract surgeries took place as long ago as the fifth century BCE. The operation took place only on cataracts that were fully mature and hardened. The operator made an incision into the eye and then pushed the cloudy lens out of place, into the vitreous chamber of the eye. Some vision was restored, but the eye could not focus well.

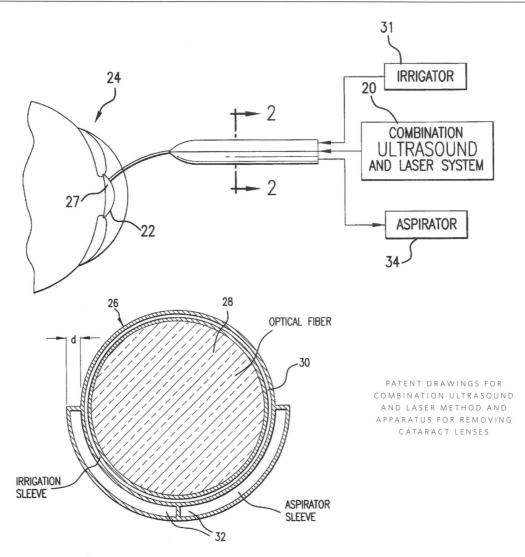

PATENT DRAWINGS FOR COMBINATION ULTRASOUND AND LASER METHOD AND APPARATUS FOR REMOVING CATARACT LENSES

For a year, Bath spent time at several European research centers, including the Laser Medical Center of Berlin, the Rothschild Eye Institute of Paris, and England's Loughborough Institute of Technology. She learned about the latest research and developments in laser technology. In Europe, her work was accepted on its merits, and she felt that she achieved her personal best in research. As she later told elementary students in Los Angeles, "Do not allow your mind to be imprisoned by majority thinking. Remember that the limits of science are not the limits of imagination."

Back at UCLA, Bath continued her experimentation with lasers, using eyes from human or animal cadavers. In 1988, after seven years of work, she earned a patent for her LaserPhaco, which stood for "laser photoablative cataract surgery." The LaserPhaco allowed a surgeon to make a one millimeter incision in the eye and to vaporize the cataract with great precision, while at the same time flushing the eye and suctioning out the remnants of the lens. The capsule around the lens was not destroyed, which allowed the surgeon to slip a new or artificial lens securely into place. Bath demonstrated use of the device and the method in the U.S. and abroad. Using the LaserPhaco, she was able to restore vision to people who had been blind for as long as thirty years. Later, reflecting back on her career, she said, "The ability to restore sight is the ultimate reward."

Despite Bath's success, she did not find immediate acceptance for her method. She told *Time* magazine that "In some instances there was anger that *petite moi,* little me, had indeed shattered the glass ceiling, had a scientific breakthrough." Perhaps as a result of this resistance, the LaserPhaco probe itself was never commercially marketed. However, the method of laser cataract surgery that Bath proposed and taught spread worldwide, restoring or improving vision for millions of people.

Following Bath's first patent, she received four more, all for improvements in the LaserPhaco. The fifth patent, issued in 2003, described a device that allowed either ultrasound pulses or laser pulses to travel along a single fiberoptic line. This allowed the operator to optimize how much energy should be delivered to different parts of the cloudy lens, which tended to be much harder and more dense in some parts than others.

Bath took pride in her identity as a scientist, clinician and inventor. "I had a few obstacles," she later told students, "but I had to shake it off. You have to ignore that and keep your eyes focused on the prize."

Meanwhile, Bath's status as professor and inventor helped her pursue her other great passion, providing preventive care to all communities. The idea of community ophthalmology, combining strategies of public health with knowledge of eye health, has spread across the world with the support of the World Health Organization. Eye health workers focus on educating people about the causes of blindness and how to prevent it. They test children to see if they need glasses, allowing them to succeed in school. They screen people who may need surgical intervention to treat blindness.

In 1993, Dr. Bath retired from the staff at UCLA. In retirement, she advocated for telemedicine, using video communication to treat patients and advise other health care workers. She practiced telemedicine both through Howard University and St. George's University on the Caribbean island of Grenada.

In 2017, the medical newsletter *Medscape* named Patricia Bath one of "Fourteen Women Physicians Who Changed the Course of American Medicine." Two years later, in 2019, Bath died of complications of cancer. Her obituary in the British medical journal *Lancet* remembered her as a pioneer: the first African American woman to become an ophthalmologist and the first to earn a medical patent.

Perhaps Bath herself said it best, embodying the spirit of all the women in this book. While acknowledging the barriers she had faced, she told *Time* magazine, "I realize that, when I achieve these things, it helps what other women, and other people of color, Black women, can do. But keep in mind...I never had any doubts."

> *"But keep in mind . . . I never had any doubts"*

AFTERWORD

What is it like to be a woman scientist today? That is the question that most often greets me as I give talks about this book, whether to schoolchildren or adults.

We can begin with the numbers. Already by 2010, 45 percent of US science PhDs and 23% of engineering PhDs were awarded to women. Slightly more than half of medical students are now women, up from three percent a century ago. In 2020, two women were awarded the Nobel Prize in chemistry for their work on the gene-editing system known as CRISPR, which has become a powerful tool for research in biology.

Still, men still dominate the upper echelons of academic science and medicine. Women start off well. They take no longer to earn a doctoral degree than men do, about 7-8 years after a bachelor's degree on average. However, women still encounter barriers to entering and rising in their profession. When researchers in 2013 sent identical resumes to professors of physics, chemistry, and biology, the professors rated the job applicants more highly if they had a male name than if they had a female name—and this happened whether the professor doing the rating was male or female. Once employed, women are still undervalued. Their earnings lag those of men, whether in science, engineering, or medicine. Perhaps as a result, they are also more likely to leave the field.

Clearly, stereotyping about who has scientific aptitude still exists throughout the academic world. For this reason, early family support for a young girl's interest in science is still as vital as ever. So are encouragement and a chance to challenge herself. Many young women in science still suffer from imposter syndrome, the feeling that they do not belong in their positions and have somehow faked their way to getting there.

Especially in male-dominated classes, laboratories or workplaces, sexist behavior and sexual harassment still exist. Women are often subject to unwanted comments on their looks or clothes, sexist jokes, and unwelcome romantic attention. Even where these are absent, women may feel pressure to be "one of the guys," accepting or participating in behavior that makes them uncomfortable—or else be labeled a "buzzkill," standoffish, unfriendly or cold. Moreover, young college women worry about a social stigma or stereotype attached to their field of study: as one young woman said, in an interview with the New York *Times*, "I hate when people in a bar or at a party find out I'm majoring in physics. The minute they find out, I can see the guys turn away."

Over the course of their careers, women in science, like women in the workplace generally, often report being ignored or passed over while they hear some of their best ideas attributed to male colleagues. In scientific meetings, women may find themselves assumed to be junior members even of teams they are leading.

Moreover, like all working women, most women in science struggle with questions of work-life balance. As has been true since at least the time of Laura Bassi, they find it vital to choose a life partner who will truly support their career. Often they build a two-academic family, requiring trade-offs, turn-taking and compromise.

Still, there is no doubt that the challenges faced by today's girls and young women present far less of a handicap to women's accomplishment than the barriers their foremothers overcame in the past. Nobody today doubts the ability of females to benefit from higher education. Role models exist. Most academic departments and technology businesses actively recruit women applicants.

Here is some of the advice women scientists offer to those following their path: Network with others in your field, especially women. In high school, college, and beyond, team up with other women to study together, share ideas, and provide encouragement. Find out about and join organizations created to allow women in science or technology to support one another. Seek out accomplished, nurturing, trustworthy mentors, female if possible. Don't hesitate to call attention to sexist behavior if and when it occurs. After finishing your studies, seek out a respectful workplace. Remember not to submit to anybody else's conception of what it means to be a woman or a scientist; instead, be as determined, joyful, independent, and courageous as the women in this book.

FURTHER READING

Bittel, Carla. *Mary Putnam Jacobi and the Politics of Medicine in Nineteenth-Century America.* Chapel Hill: University of North Carolina Press, 2009. The first full-length biography of Mary Putnam Jacobi, this book situates her in the gender politics and scientific issues of her time.

Bostridge, Mark. *Florence Nightingale: The Making of an Icon.* New York: Farrar, Straus and Giroux: 2008. There exist many biographies of Florence Nightingale, for both children and adults; this one is recent, comprehensive, and balanced.

Dunn, PM. "Louise Bourgeois (1563-1636); royal midwife of France," Archives *of Diseases of Children, Fetal and Neonatal Edition* 89: 2004, 185-187. doi: 10.1136/adc.2003.037929. Includes quotations from Bourgeois' writings and correspondence with physicians.

Essinger, James. *Ada's Algorithm: How Lord Byron's Dughter Ada Lovelace Launched the Digital Age.* New York: Melville House, 2014. A new biography for those interested in exploring more about this fascinating character.

Frize, Monique. *Laura Bassi and Science in 18th Century Europe: The Extraordinary Life and Role of Italy's Pioneering Female Professor.* Springer, 2013. Includes interesting background on the position of scholarly women in 18th century Europe.

Kovalevskaya, Sofia and Anna Carlotta Leffler. *Sonya Kovalevsky, Her Recollections of Childhood, with a Biography by Anna Carlotta Leffler, Duchess of Cajanello.* New York: The Century Co., 1895. Available on Google Books. Though somewhat disjointed, this entertaining book gives Sophie's own memories interspersed with commentary by her dear friend.

McGrayne, Sharon. *Nobel Prize Women in Science: Their Lives, Struggles, and Momentous Discoveries.* New York: Joseph Henry Press, 2001. In-depth chapters about fourteen women, including seven in this book, with sensitive accounts of their personal lives and clear explanations of their science.

Osen, Lynn. *Women in Mathematics*. Cambridge: MIT Press, 1974. Includes chapters on all the mathematical women in this book, with discussion of their work and its relation to the work of other mathematicians.

Pray, Leslie and Kira Zhaurova. "Barbara McClintock and the discovery of jumping genes (transposons)." *Nature Education* 1(1): 169, 2008. Describes McClintock's foundational experiments in some detail.

Quinn, Susan. *Marie Curie: A Life.* New York: Simon & Schuster, 1995. Again, the curious reader can find many biographies of Marie Curie, including one by her daughter, Eve; this one gives a balanced story of the passionate and dedicated scientist.

Sime, Ruth Lewin. *Lise Meitner: A Life in Physics (California Studies in the History of Science).* University of California Press, 1996. Well-researched and readable, this book delves deeply into the scientific problems Meitner investigated.

Smeltzer, Ronald K., Robert J. Ruben, and Paulette Rose. *Extraordinary Women in Science & Medicine: Four Centuries of Achievement.* New York: Grolier Club, 2013.
The source-book and inspiration for this volume, a catalogue of the exhibition of the same name at the Grolier Club in 2013.